AF886658

COMPREHENSIVE

REAL ESTATE

RESOURCE GUIDE

FAQ'S

LOAN DEFAULTS, PROPERTY REPOSITIONING & OPPORTUNITIES

By: Richard Hollowell

COMPREHENSIVE
REAL ESTATE
RESOURCE GUIDE

Abundant Press - Las Vegas, NV 89107 www.AbundantPress.com

Ordering Information & Quantity Sales: Special discounts are available on quantity purchases by corporations, associations, and others. For details, contact the publisher. Orders by U.S. & International trade bookstores and wholesalers at info@abundantpress.com. Printed in the United States of America- Library of Congress-in-Publication Data. Please note: This book was put together quickly for a conference, should you find errors, like spelling or grammar, please send us an email.

Title: Comprehensive Real Estate Resource Guide

Author: Richard Hollowell

First Edition, First Printing 8-20-2020

For more Information, visit:

RichardHollowell.com

Table of Contents

Introduction

Never before during my five-decade real estate workout career has the industry turned upside down so quickly, this time fueled by a Global Pandemic (COVID-19).

Never before have owners of hotels, shopping centers, restaurants, and office buildings had their tenants been subjected to government mandated "stay at home" orders, leading to shuttered businesses, millions of employee layoffs, and drastically reduced property rental streams. With drastically diminished cash flow, property owners face the daunting task of paying their lenders out-of-pocket, or negotiating forbearance terms or loan modifications that will provide time to bridge the health crisis and set the stage for normalcy at the property level.

For many real estate owners, they face numerous questions about how to handle this unexpected financial challenge as they decide how to approach their lender for concessions. For some, they fear that their equity is gone and they face the decision of bankruptcy, or simply turning the property back to the lender. Even worse, many borrowers face potential litigation as lenders decide whether or not to pursue enforcement actions seeking recoveries from personal guarantees.

This resource guide is designed to give **"high-level"** direction to property owners regarding many of their questions they currently face. The answers provided based upon the typical behaviors of property tenants, borrowers, guarantors, and lenders when property cash flows diminish, or are interrupted by key tenant defaults. Further, the answers are drawn from some 2,000 distressed real estate loan negotiations from both the borrowers and lenders perspectives.

Written in an interview format with the assistance of my friend and colleague Andy Broadaway, the TOP questions posed were received from borrowers with single properties, portfolio property owners, developers with projects under construction, and certain accountants and lawyers who represent these parties. Andy poses these questions in a straight-forward, understandable manner, while answers are provided from an insider's view of how banks, CMBS Special Servicers, credit companies, insurance companies, and hard money lenders look at their borrowers in distressed situations.

As we sit here in the summer of 2020, this will be my 7th real estate downturn, and each cycle was caused by a different series of events. In the 1970's it was the collapse of the mortgage REIT industry brought about by aggressive, speculative lending on everything from massive second home lot developments, to resort hotels near ski slopes near mountain ranges in the west.

In the early 1980's, developers faced a prime lending rate which ranged from 15% to 20%, followed by the infamous Tax Reform Act of 1986 which effectively eliminated favorable capital gains tax rates, as well as accelerated appreciation on commercial real estate. The real estate syndication industry was laid to rest in 1987. Then, the historic crash of the Savings & Loan Industry spanned 1986 to 1995 as 1,043 thrifts failed, causing the government to establish the Resolution Trust Corporation to liquidate real estate related assets.

That debacle was caused in great part by S&L owners who possessed limited banking experience, and favored aggressive real estate lending and property development platforms to bolster earnings and collect fees.

Few of the failed S&L owners had a sense for project feasibility or construction loan underwriting. And, of course, the systemic crash of the U.S. financial markets in 2008, which morphed into an 35% slide of commercial property values in 2009, and many millions of residential home foreclosures.

Among the chapters of this Resource Guide, the reader will learn:

- How to **best approach** a bank or CMBS Special Servicer for a loan modification.
- How to pivot in the **middle of a construction loan** under the assumption that the leasing and/or analyses conducted prior to the loan's inception are no longer valid.
- How to **reposition** a retail property that will be left with long-term vacancies post-Covid.
- The **long term affects** technology and the new found ease of working-from-home will have on the face of office buildings.
- How to find lenders and/or **opportunistic lenders** who might consider funding for a distressed property.
- How to **minimize rent concessions**, yet keep tenants in place while the world awaits a solution to the Pandemic.
- How will **appraisers determine** the value of a property for lending or investment purposes when cash flow is **severely diminished** due to the Covid lockdown, and
- When to **consider filing** a Chapter 11 bankruptcy proceeding, and when to consider turning the property over to the lender?
- When will opportunistic real estate investors be able to purchase non-performing notes or **foreclosed** properties from banks, CMBS Special Servicers, and other lenders involved in the real estate industry?

For many reasons, the face of certain real estate asset classes will forever be changed by Covid. In the **blink of an eye**, consumers have changed the way they shop, work habits have changed, the camaraderie of office gatherings is gone, and the demand for commercial real estate has dramatically changed. It is our hope that this Resource Guide will give you some high-level direction as an owner of commercial real estate. We stand ready to assist in any conflict you might have.

Who is Richard Hollowell?

Richard Hollowell has spent five decades in the real estate finance, development, loan workout, capital markets, expert testimony, and property repositioning business. He has served a broad spectrum of clients including banks, portfolio property owners, insurance companies, CMBS Special Servicers, insurance companies, pension funds, real estate hedge funds, foreign real estate owners, and government agencies including the FSLIC, RTC, and FDIC.

During his career, he has managed the evaluation, management, and resolution of over 1,500 troubled real estate loans, while assisting major developers and portfolio property owners in dealing with their lenders during troubled times.

Richard is among America's preeminent experts in restructuring troubled real estate loans, often serving lenders, but sometimes their borrowers in developing creative solutions to enhance the value of underperforming properties that serve as loan collateral.

In August 2008, he was among six national real estate experts called to speak before 20 of Federal Reserve Chairman Ben Bernanke's key staff as the systemic crash of the U.S. financial markets accelerated. He is among the top testifying experts in the country assisting both regional and national law firms in litigation cases regarding failed banks, troubled real estate, partnership disputes, lender liability, breach of fiduciary duty, and bankruptcy.

He is a widely published authority and featured speaker at real estate investment, corporate turnaround, and law conferences regarding crisis management, loan restructuring, loan securitization, capital markets, and bankruptcy.

For more Information, visit:

RichardHollowell.com

1.

What particular covenant defaults are most alarming to my lender?

Andy

Andy Broadaway here with Richard Hollowell, and real estate owners across the country unable to pay their full mortgage payment have growing concerns about covenant violations. The following question comes from a troubled property owner who asks, "What particular covenant defaults are most alarming to my lender?" This question has a borrower wondering what is in the mind of his lender and how do I align myself with the lender? Am I getting that correct?

Richard

That is correct. There are really two key covenants that your lender will be focused on these days, even if you're making your payments and maybe you are "going out of pocket" to make the payments. First is the debt service coverage ratio. As I mentioned in another interview, if you have a hundred thousand dollars in principal and interest payments and your debt coverage ratio is 1.25x, you have to show the lender $125,000 of net operating income. And when that doesn't happen, a technical default could occur if not cured. Then, the lender may be able to declare a default, accelerate repayment of the loan and start foreclosure actions. Another covenant default that lenders are looking very closely at is borrower liquidity. They are closely following whether the financial position of the borrower and/or guarantors has materially changed since the last reporting period; and, at the time the loan was made so as to consider whether you have the financial resources to carry this loan through a troubled period when income is down.

So those are the two things that they're really looking at closely as it relates to covenant defaults. Just know that as soon as you are in violation of one or more of these covenants, at the very least your loan will likely be placed on the lender's "watch list" where the surveillance on your loan is increased both in rigor and in frequency. Compliance with the loan requirements on financial reporting - both personal and at the property level - will similarly be enhanced if there was any slippage in enforcement of those loan provisions. The underlying information and documentation that is reflective in financial reports may also be "fair game" for your lender to request.

Andy

So, is this something that your team can assist with when it comes to complying with and putting these necessary reports together?

Richard

Yes Andy, as part of our work when we are brought in as an advocate for a borrower, we will review the full set of loan agreements with particular focus on all borrower covenants, and then review the relevant financial conditions of the property, the borrower and any guarantor to determine which covenants may expose you to a lender declaring a default. As an advocate, we want to be prepared when approaching the lender, knowing all the relevant facts in order to be effective. Before approaching the lender on the borrower's behalf, we want to have talked to you as the borrower or real estate owner to assess where you believe this property is going to go and where your cash flow is going to go in the short term, medium-term, and long-term. We want to help develop the most credible cash flow forecast possible; yet we appreciate that no one possesses the crystal ball as to when things will return to "normalcy" after COVID. A borrower should always want to deliver as much information as possible in an organized and integrated presentation that will expedite lender review and ultimate approval. Oftentimes it's valuable for an intermediary advocate who has sat in the lender's chair to actually deliver that restructuring proposal and presentation.

Andy

Well, that's super. In what situations do you think it's a good idea to involve someone like you in covenant default or loan restructure discussions? When is that? When does someone pick up the phone and call your office and talk to your team?

Richard

Well, I think people should be seeking an advocate as soon as they have a feeling that they don't know how the lender is going to react, whether it's a bank, a credit company, a CMBS lender, or a private money lender; if you don't have a good idea how they're going to react to the property's reduced cash flow or other such technical defaults, I firmly believe that it helps to seek out a consultant such as my firm, even if you continue to make all payments due under the loan.

Andy

Fantastic. So how do we get more information? How do we reach you and your team to specifically talk about those issues? What does the process look like?

Richard

People can reach us for a consultation at **Richardhollowell.com**. When we're in touch with you we're going to ask you for a laundry list of information, extending from your rent roll to your historic financials; in particular, your current financials, who is paying rent, who's not paying rent. We are also going to look at your loan agreements so we understand the covenants you are supposed to abide by. And we're going to look at it from the lender's perspective too, with a sense of hope that we can come to a solution with that lender so that they don't accelerate the loan and initiate foreclosure and other remedies under the loan documents.

2.

What information should I plan to submit to my lender, who I intend to approach for a loan modification or for forbearance?

Andy

Andy Broadaway and I'm here with Richard Hollowell and this is a continuation of an interview that we've broken down into very specific questions. So, the question I have for you, Richard, is "What information should I plan to submit to my lender, who I intend to approach for a loan modification or for forbearance?"

Richard

Well, that's a great question. As far as lenders are concerned, they want as much information as you can give them. The more prepared you are going to them, the smarter you're going to look as a borrower, and the more receptive they're going to be as a lender in granting a forbearance or perhaps a loan modification. I actually have an example here of a presentation we made to a CMBS special servicer a couple of years ago. We try to do the lender's work for them; as if we were analyzing the situation of that borrower, in light of the borrower's forbearance request. This presentation breaks down into a few different sections. Number one, we tell the lender everything that we have analyzed to come up with the conclusion that they're going to read in this report. So, we lay out the entire scope of work, what we looked at financially, how we looked at the operations of the property, and we set a baseline for what we did to assess the situation. Second, we outline why they are hearing from us and why we have a special situation.

Our description of the situation could include an explanation that our client has lost a couple of major tenants, or that the retail center was shut down due to COVID. Maybe the hotel has been dark and can't reopen for a few months. Our presentation is based on how the lender will look at the situation. We walk them through the current situation on a step-by-step basis. We'll update the lender on the attributes of the property, its historical performance and its competitive position in the market. We will underwrite and present what we propose as a feasible and credible strategy to bring the loan back to a performing basis and how a suggested restructure of the loan is the best way to get the lender repaid in full. We will identify the risks to the proposal's success and all mitigants.

Remember, we tackle the underwriting as if we were the lender and that requires looking at all leases, lease termination dates, market conditions, macro-economic conditions, and the past financial history of the property; we then roll up that information into a five to seven-year cash flow proforma in the form and with substance that meets lender's expectations.

You can see that there is a rigorous financial analysis that is baked into what we provide after we assess the property, its leases, and the competitive market. Before we go to the lender, we'll also do one other thing. Even though we are not appraisers, my team has collectively read thousands of commercial real estate appraisals, and we've developed a similar number of cash flow models. We understand property valuations and how to present today's and tomorrow's value to the lender. In my sample case, we asked for a three-year loan extension because the loan was maturing and we had to replace two large tenants that filed bankruptcy.

Our sample case also called for the borrower to inject new funds while it reached out to procure new tenants. Among the relevant considerations are the costs for tenant finishes, leasing commissions, free rent and other concessions that would be necessary to do so. It is our job to do the lender's analytical job for them, which will lead them to a workout conclusion that works for them and the borrower. We also tell the lender why they should not want to pursue the foreclose option and why and the how the borrower will add value to maximize repayment of the loan.

For example, why the property is best left in the hands of the owner who understands it, has made an investment, and holds meaningful relationships with the tenants. So that's the essence of the 20-page write up that we put together in a form that can easily and quickly be used for presentation to the lender's loan committee. Of course, the lender will ask us a lot of questions relative to our assumptions, and we know what the questions will be, the answers, and how these answers should be presented.

Andy

So, the process that you just talked about, this 20-page presentation that you give to the lender, how long does that typically take from an initial phone call with you and your team to a formal presentation to the lender?

Richard

Basically, we can usually get that done in three or five weeks if we have the full cooperation of the borrower; and it can be as short as three weeks, but a bit longer if it's a big complex property that is mixed-use in nature with multiple tenants. Our presentations will always include an analysis of the competitive market for each type of real estate that is part of the collateral. So perhaps we'll have to evaluate competitive retail, office, and apartment projects if it is a mixed-use property.

Andy

And I imagine that as you are working on your analysis, you are communicating with the lender on the owner's behalf. Correct?

Richard

Yes. And it's typical of the party that engages us to put the lender on notice that we've been hired, that here are our credentials and why we're the right party to put together this lender analysis. Thereafter, we'll let the lender know that "we've sat in their seat", whether they are a bank, CMBS special servicer, life insurance company, or debt fund. Regardless, we know not only what they want, but what information and analyses they need. It's good for us to start building a relationship even before the presentation is delivered and discussed.

Andy

Like in a prior interview, the question is, when do we begin that conversation? Is it before the lender starts calling you?

Richard

Absolutely, we try to tell borrowers who know that they are facing a bad situation, that denial and hiding is not a strategy. COVID is affecting everyone involved in real estate and lenders know borrowers are going to be knocking on their door, so we recommend getting there early with a presentation that is complete and puts your request on the top of the pile.

Andy

That's great. So, Richard, how do we get more information from your company on how you can help?

Richard

Property owners can contact us through **Richardhollowell.com** and populate a short form as it relates to their specific situation. We'll ask for some contact information so we can reach out to you for a short interview to see if it's something we can help with, and if we can help you bring a solution to the challenge you are facing. We may find out that we know the lender involved in your loan, which is always helpful.

3.

Are there differences in how banks and CMBS lenders and private lenders consider a problem loan situation?

Andy

Andy Broadaway here and I'm here with Richard Hollowell and this is a continuing series of interviews. And we've broken the interview process to specific questions real estate owners are asking right now. So, in prior interviews, we discussed covenant defaults, forbearance requests and loan modifications. And today's particular question is, "Richard, are there differences in how banks, CMBS lenders, and private lenders consider a problem loan situation? And, how does each look at my forbearance request?

Richard

That is a question that I get frequently because starting nearly 30 years ago, it wasn't just banks that were making real estate related loans, but lenders who entered the market to make CRE loans, after which they would bundle the loans and sell them off in securities. These bundled-loans are known as Commercial Mortgage Backed Securities. These type loans are generally non-recourse and have become a big source of financing for real estate borrowers. And then of course, you have private money lenders, which sometimes might be called hard money lenders. So, I get calls from borrowers telling me, here's the type of lender I have, how will they react when I approach them for loan forbearance or a loan modification? How will they react to my problem?

For starters banks normally have internal staff to analyze a problem loan and to try to come up with a workout solution with you. For CMBS loans, your loan is serviced by a so-called master servicer, which basically collects payments. Generally, if you fail to make payments for 60 days or you advise that you no longer have the capacity to make loan payments, your loan is transferred to a "Special Servicer," a collection agent of sorts that is highly experienced in dealing with defaulted loans.

I ran a Special Servicing firm back in the 1990s and was the President of that particular company. Employees in these special servicing companies are experts that only work on troubled loans. They have a rule book that is very specific to your CMBS loan, and somewhat similar to the comprehensive loan collection policies and procedures a bank adopts which directs their officers on how to deal with you. Having been a Special Servicer and a banker, I have knowledge of these so-called rule books and I know how they'll approach a borrower that is not paying.

I also know what it takes for them to grant a loan forbearance or a loan modification. Then you have hard money lenders, and that's a little more akin of the Wild West because hard money lenders aren't regulated like banks or CMBS lenders.

So, let's go through each type of lender for a second or two. With a bank, I previously talked about contacting your lender as soon as you know you have a problem. You'll probably be talking to your loan relationship officer, or you might be transferred to its separate commercial special asset's unit.

If you're approaching your loan relationship officer and the officer is not authorized to deal with you, the officer will likely help you transition your problem to the special asset's specialist. I've been a special assets officer at a bank, and I also was the President of an asset management company that helped the RTC and FDIC manage over 1,500 problem loans during the savings and loan crisis. So, we had a playbook as to how to react to different types of requests. On the CMBS side, the servicing industry has consolidated and today there are only 5 or 6 major special servicers and we have working relationships with virtually all of them. This May, the CMBS industry issued a guide to managing forbearance and loan modification requests, so that guide includes their general parameters as to how they'll approach your forbearance request. And, we have those guidelines so we can best help our clients.

If you're in trouble on a hard money loan, it is best for you to leverage any relationship you built at loan origination. You should be transparent upfront and explain what your strategy is to work out of the problem situation. One element all lenders have in common is that each and every one is going to want you to continue loan payments going forward even if they agree to defer payment of a portion of the payment. Each will likely want to control all your net cash flow and they'll be making sure that you'll be keeping your real estate taxes and insurance payments current. Each type of lender will also be looking to see what kind of additional investment you can make to support payment deficits. Be prepared to deliver an updated financial statement showing your current liquidity.

To support any workout proposal, your lender will ask for a comprehensive business plan and analysis of where you're at, where you're going, and where you think your financial situation will be say six months down the road, so they can decide whether forbearance is possible. Remember, you're the property owner and you need to confidently put forth a strategy that is feasible and is reflective of your added value as a knowledgeable and competent owner; then you must be able to execute that strategy. In essence, when you obtain the forbearance or a loan modification, you'll be graded against your plan.

Andy

It sounds like this is something that your team is not only trained to handle, but you personally have almost 50 years of experience. So, Richard, I've been taking notes and essentially you used the word playbook several times. And it seems that you have knowledge of the playbooks that lenders use, and that you talk their language, is that correct?

Richard

Yes, Andy, that's correct. And, we understand the idiosyncrasies of each type of loan, remembering that banks normally require their borrowers to provide personal guarantees. That issue alone sheds a special light on your loan situation and how the lender will try to maximize its collection. Having sat in the lender's chair for years upon years, we are well equipped to be an advocate for borrowers.

Andy

Well, that's great to know. So how do we get more information regarding working with you and your team? What are the first steps that we need to take and then let's wrap up this interview?

Richard

The way to get in touch with us is to go to **Richardhollowell.com** and put a short story about your situation on the form you'll find on our landing page. We will take a look at your situation and either I or one of our senior consultants will get back to you. Again, just go to **Richardhollowell.com**.

4.

I've got a decision to make, do I default on the loan or do I try to find someone to bail me out of my situation?

Andy

Andy Broadaway here and I'm with Richard Hollowell discussing the way Covid-19 is affecting commercial real estate. Today, I have a very unique question for you. It comes from a hotel owner who says, "I don't see my hotel occupancy and average daily rate being similar to what I achieved in 2018 and 2019 for quite a while; and, I don't have the money to keep my loan payments current. Do I just throw in the towel, or is there any kind of alternative out there for me?" So, Richard how do you address what seems to be a very dire situation, can you and your team help?

Richard

Andy, I fear that many hotel and retail shopping center owners are going to be asking themselves that question in the very near future. The first answer to this question is to determine if the principal of the borrowing entity has personally guaranteed the loan or not. If it is a CMBS loan, the loan is non-recourse unless the borrower's principal has violated a bad-boy covenant and triggered a springing guarantee. If it is a bank or insurance company loan where personal guarantees are often required, the analysis is different. To lay some foundation, going back to the real estate down cycles of the '80s, 90's, then the great recession, I've become acquainted with many opportunistic real estate investors that might step in to help a distressed borrower. Often, they take the form of a family office or a so-called real estate opportunity fund.

There are folks in that business all over the country and I've worked with some significant parties in New York, Chicago, Miami, and Los Angeles, and there are often private investors in the local market where the property is that might jump in. Often, they'll approach the lender to buy the mortgage, then restructure it and convert it to paying loan, leaving the original owner a piece of equity on a negotiated basis. If the borrower is to the point of throwing in the towel, we can look at the situation and the property to see if we can arrange for an investor. When that happens, we'll need to persuade the lender to go along with the strategy that avoids foreclosure and/or potential personal liability, and that's where hard negotiations play out.

I actually just had this kind of call about three weeks ago when a group that I've known for years called me. This group has assembled quite a bit of money to buy troubled real estate and they asked me to do some due diligence on a 300-unit apartment building in LA, which is half-built, and where construction has stopped. They were not sure how to approach the owner, or whether they should go straight to the lender and asked me for direction.

Based upon this particular case where construction has stopped and the property needs another $15 million to complete, I coupled that information with the fact that the lender is a foreign entity, and I recommended that we go straight to the lender. We will be making an offer the buy the note (loan) at a discount, primarily based on a cost to complete study we put together to justify the offered price. If successful, we'll then approach the borrower to see if we can keep them in the deal for a small slice and finish up the project. Their project knowledge will likely be helpful and we'll avoid foreclosure through that method.

So, I've given many speeches over the last 20 years at real estate opportunity fund conferences; many of these conferences had more than 1,000 attendees. So, if borrowers are ready to throw in the towel, perhaps we can enlist one of the investors we know to help out.

Andy

Well, fantastic. I'm glad that you're there as a resource to those people who have reached the end of their rope. But, what about folks that have a personal guarantee, you mentioned that the analysis for those people is a bit different, please tell me about that kind of situation.

Richard

The best way for me to describe how we help borrowers in that situation is to give you a historical case example going back to 2011. I was approached by a real estate developer who was very successful back in the 1980's and 1990's in the shopping center business. He decided somewhere around 2006 that he wanted to build waterfront condominiums in Florida, something he had never done before. So, he purchased a $20 million land parcel suited for a 20-story condominium. He put $6 million down and borrowed $14 million supported by his personal guarantee. Before he could get his project started the market collapsed during the Great Recession, and the value of the property decreased to around $5 million; he was personally on the hook for the entire loan.

As his shopping centers were not performing well due to the recession, he actually had five lenders chasing him for money and threatening to foreclose. My approach was to prepare a "liquidation analysis" of what each lender would realize if we had to have the borrower file a Chapter 7 liquidation plan. Then, we used that analysis to go to the land lender in Florida, and we settled his $14 million personal guarantee obligation for $900,000, plus an agreement not to contest a foreclosure action. Of course, that is an over-simplified version of a case that took four months, but we got our client out of a trap.

In most cases where a personal guarantee is involved, we can prepare a bankruptcy liquidation business analysis, then we go to each lender, one by one, to orchestrate a global settlement for the client. I see my group using that process frequently in the months to come, particularly on construction loans which will have no takeout loan, and where the developer has a personal guarantee. As testifying experts in bankruptcy court, we're very effective talking to lenders.

Andy

What an interesting story Richard, how can real estate borrowers contact you to tell you more about their particular situation?

Richard:

If you're somebody that has a real challenge as I've described above, and can't decide how to go forward with a property, you can go to our website at **www.Richardhollowell.com**. Once there, you'll find a confidential form you can populate with specifics on the financial challenge you face. We'll set up a consultation and see if it's something we think we can help solve. Maybe we can help build a bridge to a better day, and avoid a bankruptcy proceeding. Again, the website is **www.Richardhollowell.com.**

5.

Knowing what you know about banks and CMBS servicers, what challenges are they having?

Andy

Andy Broadaway here, and I'm with Richard Hollowell addressing a host of questions real estate owners are now asking themselves due to the adverse effects of the Covid stay-at-home order. Richard, "Knowing what you know about Banks and CMBS Special Servicers, what challenges are they currently having?"

Richard

Great question Andy. Many real estate borrowers who finance their properties with Banks or CMBS Lenders don't really understand what's going on inside their bank or loan servicer when a multitude of their borrowers stop making payments at once. As loan defaults were near all-time lows before Covid hit, lenders were totally unprepared for the surge of loan forbearance requests. So, the popular saying that "we're all in this together," is quite true. The CMBS special servicers and the special assets departments of banks, are in this up to their eyeballs right now with calls from their borrowers. Let me give you an example; I was talking to the Southern California special assets representative for a top 25 bank around May 1, 2020; he has to address all the non-paying real estate loans in the Southern California area. Literally, he's on the phone with borrowers, he hands out receiverships in cases where he's foreclosing, he works on modifications, and he works on forbearance requests. So, until he finds more help, he's a one-man-band who could literally work 30 hours per day.

I've been through six real estate down cycles and never before did I see lenders with literally few non-performing loans, then overnight a literal flood occurs. Staffing-up with bankers who have skill sets in dealing with troubled loans will be tough, as many of the experts that worked on troubled loans during the Savings & Loan crisis of 1988 to 1995 and the Great Recession of 2008 to 2011 are no longer in the workout business, or retired. So, if you're calling your bank to ask for forbearance and you're having trouble getting through, now you know why. As for CMBS Special Servicers, they're in the same boat as banks. I've talked to some of my contacts in the Special Servicing business and they tell me that every asset manager is getting 10 new troubled loans to work on every day. So how does an asset manager deal with that volume until they hire more people?

As someone who was the national President of a Special Servicing company that employed 175 full time people, I can tell you that it take a few days to do a preliminary triage of each file, let alone getting together with your borrower, his consultants, and possibly his lawyer to determine if a loan forbearance or modification package is justified. Remember, if you have a loan that's been placed with a Special Servicer on Monday morning, he's going to have another 40-50 new loans to work on by the end of the week. Both banks and special servicers are frantically trying to staff up now.

So, I tell the borrowers you must be proactive in developing a strategy and put it in front of your lender as soon as possible. That strategy should be well thought out, well documented, and put in a clear format that tells the lender the full story, including what you're requesting. The more complete your strategy is and the more comprehensive your support is for your proposal, the better chance you have that your proposal will be advanced to the loan committee for approval.

So, do as much of the lender's work as you can to bring the officer up to speed, don't make him start from scratch when you make your request. Make sure your presentation summarizes the (i) background and original purpose of the loan, (ii) what the original underwriting looked like and initial loan metrics such as DSCR and LTV (iii) what your trailing-12 month cash flow looked like with explanation for all sources of revenue and expenses, (iv) why you need a forbearance, (v) what is your strategy to get your payments back on track, (vi) whether you are willing to commit additional money to fund cash flow deficits, and (vii) why the lender should leave you in charge of the property as opposed to putting it in the hands of a court-appointed receiver.

You may also want your analysis to explain why leaving your management uninterrupted will maximize collection on the loan. You should include an operating forecast in the form of a net present value calculation, a standard analytical approach for lenders, then comparing the results with the foreclosure scenario. Those are just some of the issues we address when we help borrowers come up with loan modification strategies.

Andy

What I'm hearing you say here is that there is an incredible lack of skilled professionals to deal with troubled loans. And that if I'm a borrower who needs to go to his lender, I better have a well-documented plan. And I know that's a sweet spot for your firm, helping real estate owners come up with well-documented workout strategies that effectively document the request just like the lender would, correct?

Richard

That's correct. We help prepare "committee ready" presentations that will garner a quick reaction from your lender. You don't want your loan sitting on the bottom of a pile while you're unable to generate the cash flow to make your full payment. Remember, once the lender receives our request, he'll go through a quality control process to see if he agrees with our strategy, then he reacts, so you want to get started on this process at the earliest possible date.

Andy

Well, for me, I'd rather be at the front of the line than the back of the line all day long. So, I mean, working with your company and having you help put together and document a strategy is a great idea. So, Richard, how do we get more information from your company? What's the process look like? What are some of the initial steps?

Richard

For a property owner that has a challenge, there's actually a form on our website a person can populate which asks them to explain their challenge to us. Then we will set up a consultation to see if that's something that we might help with. One thing we'll promise is that we'll assess your situation, we'll tell you how the lender will react to your problem, then help develop a plan that we believe will work. Often, borrowers don't like what we're telling them, but we will always be honest as we've sat in the lender's chair over the years. And by way of disclosure, we are not always successful. But we know what's in the lenders playbook and we will always do our best to come up with a solution that works for all parties. So real estate owners can review our qualifications and those of our team members at **www.Richardhollowell.com.**

6.

Can I expect my lender to reappraise the value of my property due to COVID?

Andy

Andy Broadaway here and welcome back Richard. This is a series of interviews involving the negative impact the COVID quarantine is having on commercial real estate. So, the question I have for you today Richard is, "How and when will my lender reevaluate the value of my property due to COVID?"

Richard

That's a great question, Andy, and perhaps the toughest question facing borrowers and lenders today. To directly answer your question, lenders aren't just going to run right out and reappraise your property. If you are already in a forbearance period, which probably means you're making all or a major part of your payments, a reappraisal will likely not be required. With respect to loans that are performing, the issue that triggers a re-appraisal is when you stop making payments and your lender issues a 60-day notice of default. At that point the lender needs to assess what their exposure might be if they have to foreclose.

So today, think about the challenge the appraiser faces when properties aren't trading because of the COVID slowdown. Remember, appraisers use comparable property sales, and the properties used as comparable to the subject and usually at stabilized occupancy. That's one method used to assess the value of your property. But, what if your property and all the comparable properties are now 40% vacant; how do you arrive at value then? Well, I've been polling quite a few MAI certified appraisers as of late. And one of them said to me, "Richard, being an appraiser right now is like being an airline pilot flying a jetliner, and you're flying along at 20,000 feet and preparing for landing in 30 minutes; all of a sudden, all your flight instruments go dark, city lights go out, and there are no landing lights.

Oh, and the air traffic control system goes down as well." Simply, the appraiser doesn't have reliable data to use in the current environment. So, there's a real challenge that lenders are going to have when it comes to reappraisal. I think that's an issue that we're going to see probably for up to 18 months, and I would not be surprised to see the advent of lender liability lawsuits down the line, spawned by major disagreements between lenders and borrowers as to collateral value when they are trying to come up with ways to restructure loans. And of course, appraisers have to be very careful when they give value opinions for the foreseeable future because they must abide by USPAP standards, and use "crystal ball" as they forecast when a property will again achieve stabilized occupancy.

Andy

That makes a lot of sense and I actually liked the analogy you used about the airline pilot. And I definitely would not want to be on that plane when all the lights go out. I can see why appraisers are going to have such a big problem as they don't have reliable data to use. So, if they have poor data points, then how do they evaluate a property, in this current situation?

Richard

Well, some lenders are actually asking appraisers for three indications of value. One is pre-COVID based upon the income stream a property had in 2019. The second property value they ask for is value based upon the vacancies caused by COVID, and the third value is the post-COVID value where the appraiser has to project when the market returns to normal, and when net operating income gets to a stabilized level. Obviously, the third value will require a well-tuned crystal ball to arrive at all the metrics that get baked into a discounted cash flow analysis. And it's interesting, I've seen this problem before.

In 2008, I was called with five other professionals to speak in front of 20 of Ben Bernanke's key people at the Federal Reserve in Washington D.C. That was a three-hour session, about 30 days before Lehman filed for bankruptcy on September 15, 2008. We spent a solid hour of that particular session discussing how appraisers were going to be challenged considering that property values were starting to decline on a rapid basis. The solution that was arrived at was that appraisers would put a value on a property, but include a "Special Limiting Condition" in the appraisal which said that the appraisal and its indicated value was only valid for 90 days. So, if you started a loan restructure process that lasted more than 90 days, you would have to go back to square one and get the appraiser to revisit value before you closed the restructured loan.

Andy

Well, I have a follow-up question to that. You said that back in 2008, property values were declining at a rapid pace. What is your opinion of how values have declined due to COVID?

Richard

The decline in property values we saw in 2008 were primarily in residential properties, then it spread to commercial properties early in 2010, so it depends what asset class you're talking about. Multifamily hasn't been that affected, neither has industrial. In fact, in June 2020, the Industrial REIT's were the best performing REIT's in the real estate category. The asset class that has really been affected has been hospitality. I've talked to probably 20 of the top hotel experts in the country, including huge ownership groups, as well as a host of hotel vulture funds that have already formed funds to buy distressed hotels. The general consensus is that hotel values are down about 30% as of July 2020. And I know in my own neighborhood, one of the premier luxury hotels oriented to business travelers probably will not re-open until 2021. Then retail comes next and those values are probably down about 20% now.

So, if a shopping center owner obtained a 75% loan to value just a year or even two years ago, their equity may be pretty much wiped out. So much thought is being given to alternative uses for portions of shopping center properties to address the fact that retail bricks and mortar demand will continue on its pre-Covid downward trend after the Covid crisis is over. Repositioning may be the only way to rebuild the equity an owner had in his retail property.

Andy

And so repositioning, that's something that you and your team can help with as part of a plan to keep your existing loan in place, or find a new one?

Richard

Yes, we provide consultation in that area as we've had to reposition troubled retail centers numerous times before in our role as a court-appointed receiver. And when we're called in to provide that help, we do it considering what a lender will say when we go in for a loan modification or for new financing. Simply, we have to support the repositioning plan with an eye to feasibility, market demand and existing supply, construction timing and cost and local competition.

Andy

I think that's what's very unique about you and your team. You've seen so many different types of real estate challenges over your 50-year career, and your collective team members give your group a total of 175 years of experience, right?

Richard

That's correct Andy, we've assembled quite the dream team of senior professionals that have spent their entire careers working with troubled commercial and residential projects, so there is a lot of wisdom there. And it's interesting, one of my colleagues said today, "Knowledge is knowing that a tomato is a fruit, wisdom is knowing not to put it in a fruit salad." And that's the kind of wisdom a property owner should be seeking.

Andy

I liked that. I don't think I will ever look at a tomato the same way again after that story. And I've never even thought about that. Because there's always that argument, tomato, vegetable, fruit, vegetable, fruit going back and forth, but you just put it in a really clear perspective. That's great. So where can we find out more information on how to potentially work with your team and what kind of clients are you specifically looking to work with, where's your sweet spot?

Richard

Folks can go to www.**Richardhollowell.com** to review our qualifications and the different disciplines that we focus on. We are very effective in helping owners that hold underperforming properties, particularly those that have a challenge with their lender.

And on the flip side of that, we've done a lot of counseling for banks, for CMBS lenders and specialty lenders. Not only in our capacity as testifying experts, but also as court-appointed receivers, and liquidators of notes or foreclosed properties. Again, folks can connect with us at www.**Richardhollowell.com.**

7.

Am I in trouble if my loan matures within the next 12 months and the lending industry still hasn't rebounded from the shock of COVID?

Andy

Andy Broadaway here and I'm here with Richard Hollowell and this is a continuing interview series regarding real estate loan covenant defaults, and challenges facing commercial property owners. And this is yet another question that I wanted to ask you, and that is, "Am I in trouble if my loan matures within the next 12 months and the lending industry still hasn't rebounded from the shock of COVID?"

Richard

Well, not many people are asking this yet, but those that have maturing loans in the next 12 months are starting to address this particular issue because their cash flows are down and lenders want to be paid back in accordance with the timetable that was originally agreed to. Already, Borrowers may have received the first loan maturity notice reminding them that the loan matures in 12 months and that preparation should be made to pay off the loan at the future maturity date. A borrower could receive similar notice letters at 9 months and 6 months and monthly thereafter.

Now here's the Catch 22. I think refinancing a commercial real estate loan is going to be very difficult for the next 12 months for a few reasons. I don't believe that normalcy will return to the hotel industry, the office building industry, to retail centers, and to student housing until we have a vaccine for COVID and sufficient people have received the vaccine to achieve herd immunity. There is going to be a lot of hesitancy for consumers to get back into the market, and of course, we all know that the consumer is 70% of this economy. To go back out and have the same spending patterns at these commercial properties that they once did won't happen until we have that penetration of the vaccine in the general population.

So if I as a borrower have a loan that's maturing and it's 12 months out, I'm probably not going to address that with the lender yet, but I better start thinking out a plan to address the maturity with my existing lender within several months of maturity. In the months ahead, a borrower should be vigilant to make sure that there are no monetary or covenant missteps including compliance with all reporting requirements. I think your best source of financing once your loan terms-out is to stay with your current lender. It's not preferred in a perfect world. Everybody wants to refinance at a lower interest rate, but if you don't have the proven cash flow to go out there and get that loan refinanced, your best option is to stay with your lender. That's not a bad thing as a CMBS lenders will consider a short extension when your loan approaches maturity, but they're going to be particularly hard on you. They may want you to reduce the loan balance, add funds to reserves, or ask for other concessions or representations. As to new lenders, they'll have the challenge of getting an appraisal that they can rely on. I believe an earlier interview covered the challenges appraisers have when trying to determine market value for loan purposes.

Since the real estate market has been shocked by COVID with closures of all types of properties, getting an appraisal for a new loan request is going to be difficult. So, I think people need to build a bridge with their current lender, with the prospect that you may have to present a loan extension request. You need to be conscious of that early on so that as the maturity date approaches you are fully prepared to present updated and full underwriting support for the credit decision to extend the loan term for another year or 18 months; thereby, bridging your cash flow gap until you can achieve recovery from the effects of COVID.

Andy

That's a great strategy. What is another specific strategy when it comes to having a lender conversation; we've covered this in other interviews and being proactive in that conversation and calling the lender way before they're calling you, how important do you think that is specifically when facing a loan maturity?

Richard

Well, the most urgent issue that people are facing is gaining a forbearance package or gaining a loan modification to bridge the ramp-up of tenancies. I think that to start talking to your lender about a loan maturing in 12 months is premature; why, because you've got to walk before you run, and you need to bridge yourself to that conversation and show that you can perform on a loan that has been worked out either under a forbearance or modification for a short period of time. So, I wouldn't necessarily bring up a loan renewal or extension at the 12-month mark. I think that would be a mistake because, among other things, intervening events will affect your lender's receptivity for the renewal/extension and the terms you can present and support. Furthermore, I would expect that the lender would appreciate that the loan will continue to perform in all respects according to its current terms and conditions today and during the COVID rebound period.

Andy

Well, it sounds like your team knows how to determine when a lender should be approached and how to strategically manage the loan extension process. Do how do property owners enlist your help? Does that begin with a call to your office and you asking a series of questions regarding where everything stands with their loan? You know, are they behind on payments, are they been making partial payments, what it all looks like, and it really all begins with that conversation. Am I correct?

Richard

In that initial conversation, we'll definitely be asking the question, when does your loan mature, and when can the lender ask to be paid in full because remember, they do not have to renew your loan, even if you're making payments and have no covenant defaults? So those are issues we're going to discuss during that initial conversation before we try to assess your prospects for a loan renewal and its possible terms and conditions. We then assess how long an extension beyond the scheduled maturity date we can credibly request, and how do we plan for that.

So, folks can reach us at **www.Richardhollowell.com** and set up a short consultation with myself or with one of our four senior consultants.

8.

My construction loan is not in default, construction is progressing but, what should I be thinking about now as construction nears completion?

Andy

Andy Broadaway here, and again, I'm with Richard Hollowell and this is part of a series of interviews on the way commercial real estate is being affected by the Covid-19 pandemic. And the question that came in today goes like this, "My construction loan is not in default and construction is progressing on schedule, what should I be thinking about now as I will soon finish construction?

Richard

That's a good question and one that's coming frequently from developers that have hotels, shopping centers, multifamily and office buildings under construction right now. And before I go into an answer for the specific question, let's first look at approximately how much construction is actually going on in each asset class.

First, some 220,000 hotel rooms were under construction in April according to STR. That's the equivalent of building 575 hotels the size of the Four Seasons Hotel in Manhattan. So, adding another 220,000 rooms over the next 18-24 months will put even more stress on the already limping hotel industry. The major construction markets for hotels at this time are New York City, Dallas, Houston, Atlanta, and Nashville. Consequently, watch for stress in those markets as hotel construction is completed.

Second according to CoStar Data, there was just under 80 million square feet of retail centers under construction nationally in 2019. That's the equivalent of 80 enclosed mall regional shopping centers as we knew them back in the 1980's. The top markets for retail space construction are Houston, Northern New Jersey, Long Island, Dallas and Miami. Given the trend away from bricks and mortar retail caused not only by COVID but by the explosion of on-line retail sales, real estate opportunity funds will be looking to those top-5 markets for buying opportunities in the months to come.

Third, 371,000 apartment units are readying for delivery in 2020 according to real estate analytics from RealPage. Further, according to the Multi-Housing News, new apartment projects started in 2020 are concentrated in Denver, Fort Worth, North Dallas, Phoenix, and Austin. And of course, many know that there was an extraordinary supply of new apartments completed in New York City, Brooklyn and Queens in 2017 and 2018. In those New York markets, landlords are already feeling the negative effects of tenant flight to the suburbs to escape the central business district areas. To make the situation more challenging, of the projects slated for delivery in 2020, 80% are of the luxury variety and not affordable to the average American.

Fourth, there was approximately 110 million square feet of office space under construction in 2019 according to National Real Estate Investor. The top cities for that construction are Charlotte, Austin, Nashville, and Brooklyn. In other interviews on the office asset class, we discussed likely downsizing of offices, subleasing challenges being felt by landlords, and companies leaving the CBD for suburban locations. Hence, with some companies planning to drastically adjust their need for office space in favor of the work-from-home opportunity, you can get a sense of where some opportunities might be.

So now to your question Andy. Regardless of the type of property you have that's under construction, I recommend you immediately study your original business plan, leasing assumptions, appraisal, and any feasibility study that was done before construction commenced. There you should find all of the assumptions upon which you built your operating proforma, and from which you sized your loan. Ask yourself, what financial and leasing assumptions need to be changed due to Covid, what are competitive projects doing to attract tenants as influenced by Covid, how long will it take to achieve stabilized occupancy, and will I be able to secure permanent financing sufficient to pay off my construction lender. You'll totally need to rebuild your proforma with a very sharp pencil, then get a feasibility analyst who specializes in your asset class to test your assumptions. Be realistic with your assumptions based upon the timetables you now face, and prepare in advance to go to your construction lender and request that they stick with you under the assumption that you'll need more time to build your cash flow to an amount sufficient to attract a takeout lender.

Andy

Now, is that something that your organization and your team can strategically put together in the interest in approaching the lender?

Richard

Sure Andy, we work with the owner to document what future cash flow is going to be and assess when we believe we'll generate cash flow sufficient to secure a takeout loan. The process will include some significant analysis of how the market has changed and what it will take to secure a takeout loan. Our real estate team has been conducting due diligence and building proformas for about 150 years, and usually, we're a great liaison between the developer and lender in delivering a plan that makes everyone whole.

Andy

Well, that sounds like a great solution for someone that owns a property that is in the middle of the construction and needs a plan to complete and lease a project leading to a new takeout loan. So, what's the best way to communicate with you, Richard?

Richard

Developers that have a project under construction can reach us at www.**Richardhollowell.com**. Our qualifications are on our website and they'll find that we specialize in construction lending and the risks that go with it. There isn't much we haven't analyzed in repositioning construction loans, as we've even been put in charge of building-out a variety of projects where construction had stopped. Of first order, keep the project on budget with sufficient funds not yet disbursed to complete the project on schedule. Then when you have that side of things under control, we would be happy to discuss the balance of your challenges. Developers can find us at **www.Richardhollowell.com**, and we'll set up an initial consultation.

9.

The value of my property has dropped due to the COVID and I am in violation of my debt coverage ratio requirements. Am I at risk of foreclosure?

Andy

Andy Broadaway back and I'm here with Richard Hollowell and in the prior interview, we've talked about covenant defaults, and approaching your lender for a loan modification. In this particular interview, we're going to talk about, and specifically, the question before me is this, "The value of my property has dropped due to the COVID shutdown and I am in violation of my debt coverage ratio." Am I at risk of foreclosure? I'm sure that question is on the top of the list for many property owners right now. What are your thoughts, Richard?

Richard

Andy, it's not only violations of debt service coverage ratios, but loan-to-value ratios that property owners are worried about. It's important because if you listen to certain the industry experts they say that hotel values have declined 35%, while retail center values have gone down 20% and office values 10%. Then the experts talk about specialty classes of real estate like student housing and senior housing being down probably 20% with a default rate of about 17% on loans that have those type properties for collateral. We have developed turnaround plans for all those real estate types in the past. So, the question people are asking is valid, "Will they be pushed into foreclosure because property value went down?" Now the short answer to that is this, lenders make loans to get paid back, not to own real estate. They really don't want to own your real estate, especially when it's challenged with vacancy problems.

Lenders face "mark-to-market' issues with regulators or bondholders at the point of foreclosure, so they would rather not foreclose on you. They'd rather work out some kind of a solution to restructure your loan. But you must approach them with a realistic forward-looking business plan, showing them your current situation, when you believe you can stabilize cash flow and how, and show them you have liquidity to fund operating shortfalls over the short term if it comes to that. The plan has to show the lender how and when they can expect to get repaid at an acceptable point once it agrees to your proposed strategy. Remember they prefer not to own your property, but you better be prepared to submit to the same rigorous underwriting standards to justify your plan, then you submitted to when you originally sought the loan.

Andy

And that makes a lot of sense that lenders are not in the property ownership business, they're in the loan business. And so that's where you come along and give your clients hope because you have lived in the lender's seat before and know how to develop restructuring options that align with the lender's objective of getting paid back. And we've talked about how difficult it is to put a value on a property today, so wouldn't a lender be hesitant to declare a loan default because he thinks the value has decreased? Am I correct?

Richard

It's very difficult if not impossible to put an accurate value on any property today; literally appraisers are scratching their heads. And if I go back to 2008, when I was in a room with 20 of Federal Reserve Chairman Ben Bernanke's key people and four or five other industry experts, the big issue that was addressed for a full hour out of the three-hour meeting, was how do you appraise a property when values are going down rapidly? That was a very difficult discussion and there were some high-level appraisal people in that room.

That spawned a special clause that we ended up seeing in many appraisals which basically said, here's the market value in our opinion today, but this market value is only valid and may be relied upon only for 90 days, as market conditions and the financial returns at the property level are changing. And so, we saw this "special limiting condition" show up in appraisals that simply made the appraisal an invalid indication of value in three months. Appraisals right now, and really for the next 12 months, are going to be very difficult to rely on as it relates to what the value is from day to day for commercial property. That is why I had mentioned before that some appraisers are looking at three values, (i) a pre-COVID value, (ii) a value today as affected by COVID non-paying tenants, and (iii) a market value at stabilization. In making that last determination, the appraiser is asked to predict when occupancy will again be stabilized and on what rent and other lease terms.

Andy

That brings up another question. One of the case studies you talked about on camera involved your working with a mall owner that lost two of its largest tenants. So, in a situation like that, how does someone assess the market value?

Richard

Well here's what we did for that particular individual, and he lost two of his anchor tenants almost simultaneously, severely disrupting his cash flow. Fortunately, this was a developer that was the preeminent developer of shopping centers in his market and he knew who all the prospective tenants would be for his center. The owner offered to infuse more money into the project while he attracted new tenants to the vacant spaces, he agreed to subdivide spaces for new tenants without touching the leasing reserves that the lender maintained, he agreed to bring the loan current, and he agreed to manage the property without earning a property management fee. He also agreed to replace the tenants he had lost within one year.

So, we asked the lender for an interest rate modification, and for the lender split the loan note into what we call A and B pieces. The B note carried a below-market pay rate, but gave the lender a 50% preferred equity position when the property was sold or refinanced. Even though the current loan to value was 100%, that loan restructure was successful and the lender was paid in full 2 1/2 years later, including a return on its 50% residual equity.

Andy

Well, I think that was very creative, and is that typical of the way you approach all loan restructures? We started this interview with real estate owners fearing that they would be foreclosed on due to covenant defaults and the fact that value of their properties has decreased.

Richard

Andy, every loan workout situation is different, so there is not a cookie-cutter approach to each assignment. There is quite a bit of analysis that goes into devising a workout proposal that will fit a specific lender, and remember, different lenders may play by different internal rules.

As I orchestrated loan workouts from my Florida office in the past, I actually decided to publish an article called "Befriending your lender in troubled times." This was back around 9/11 when the aviation industry down in South Florida was falling apart. And I wrote that there's no substitute for being transparent with your lender and getting to them early with a well-documented workable strategy to get them paid back. But you have to befriend them early in the process; as soon as you have a sense of what your problem is and how you will solve it. Lenders are reluctant to foreclose a conscientious borrower.

Andy

That's great. So, you and your team can work for a borrower and open an early line of communication that will buy the real estate owner some time to put together a plan, correct?

Richard

Yes, we are a credible intermediary that can initiate a dialogue with a lender even before the lender initiates a call. We make sure the lender knows that the client is not ignoring the problem situation; that we are working proactively on a plan that we will present, that will develop a plan that meets the lender's credit decision-making standards within a promised time frame. Whether we are hired or the borrower initiates that call, perhaps through its CFO, I stress to get to the lender early.

Andy

Wonderful. That's good to know. So, Richard, how do we get more information? What's the process on how a prospective client starts working with you? And also, who is your typical client?

Richard

Typically, we don't get involved at the homeownership level. Rather, we've worked on loans that have ranged from $5 million to $200 million on all types of properties around the country. So, if you have a loan challenge in that dollar amount range, those are the types of assignments that are in our sweet-spot and we've probably worked on over 1,000 assignments in that range. So, we know the questions to ask you and we know the questions your lender's going to ask, and how to answer those questions in a persuasive way.

Andy

Wonderful. So, what's the best way to reach your office and how do we set up a consultation call?

Richard

Well, the best way is to reach out to us at **www.Richardhollowell.com** and set up a short consultation either with myself or with one of my four senior consultants, collectively with over 150 years of real estate loan workout experience.

10.

What factors should I consider when my tenants are asking for rent concessions?

Andy

Andy Broadaway here and I'm here with Richard Hollowell and in the prior interviews, we've asked questions about being in covenant default, foreclosures, and bankruptcies. We've discussed how a real estate borrower opens a conversation and dialogue with their lender on those subjects. So, here's an interesting question, and I'm sure this is being asked by a lot of property owners. That is, "What factors should I consider when my tenants are asking for rent concessions?"

Richard

That's a great question, Andy, because we are now in an era of forbearance requests; and, it doesn't matter if it's a borrower that has a lender that has declared a loan default or a tenant who can't pay rent. I'm very familiar with this situation because I've been a court-appointed receiver over a dozen times, and my receivership role places me into the position of the owner, dealing with tenants with problems. And as you know, a property receiver typically doesn't get appointed unless there's a foreclosure action. As a receiver, I would put on the ownership hat and address the situation with each and every tenant. Usually when a receiver comes in and takes over control, tenants come out in full force, asking for concessions, and asking what are you going to do to improve this property? They tell you that they can't make their full rent payment. They ask you to cut it back. In response, I must undertake a financial analysis of each and every one of the tenants, what they're asking for, and what their true financial situation is to determine if I, acting essentially as the owner should enforce the existing lease terms, sue them for collection or eviction, or modify their lease.

Some of the considerations that are identified and analyzed are the same as those a property owner would be faced with. There are four or five key points. First, and using retail as an example, what has the sale revenue been of that tenant and what has been their payment history for the last 12 months. Then I focus on what's been going on the last 90 days considering what might be the seasonal nature of the business. Then I ask myself, "Is it a level of sales that actually supports the lease as was underwritten at the point of the original lease?" "What kind of personal guarantee might be backing the lease obligations of the tenant?" So, we'll want to assess the financial condition of the guarantor to see if that creates leverage for you.

We'll take this question a step further as I was once the receiver of a 300,000 square foot Oceanfront mall in Florida, and that property had virtually every problem known to man. When I was appointed as receiver, I quickly learned that it was nearly impossible to attract replacement tenants. That realization brings up the question, "what do you want to do? Kick out somebody that's paying 25% of their rent only to have one more vacant space.

Do you want to sue them to collect? Or do you want to keep them in occupancy on some kind of basis?" If you don't have tenants lined up who want to lease space, you really need to assess the "go dark" damage that you as a property owner could be exposed to if all of a sudden, you have many "For Lease" signs in storefronts without new tenants who want to be there. Furthermore, if you do have a chance to attract a few new tenants, you need to evaluate the cost going to be to bring those tenants in by having to incur the cost of tenant finishes that you are often asked to provide, free rent or other concessions, and/or leasing commissions.

Often, there will be a leasing commission with an outside broker who procures new tenants. I faced high tenant improvement costs and leasing commissions many times as a receiver, and sometimes you'll choose to keep tenants paying a compromised rental rate instead of paying the high costs for a new tenant. So, you really have to go through a forensic analysis of each tenant to determine their ability to earn their way out of the problem they are currently experiencing so that they can resume full rent payments. You are weighing alternative courses of action for each tenant and each space that could go vacant.

Andy

So, these are tough questions facing property owners; can you offer assistance on the analytical side of the equation? So as a specialist in this area, should a property owner be giving you a call just to let you handle this?

Richard

Well, if an owner doesn't have the depth and bandwidth of resources to do multiple analyses at once, even acknowledging that no one knows the property better than the owner, we can help with tenant and leasing analyses as the case might require. We'll rely on the owner for a brain dump of what the owner knows about competitive properties, and we'll look to see what analyses have already been done. So, we work closely with the owner to develop a strategy for each tenant, and looking forward to developing a strategy that will bring a property up to stabilized occupancy at the highest rents possible. We'll also consider issues such as tenant-mix, the spatial needs of the tenant and foot-traffic as part of the process.

Andy

Right-on super Richard. So, what's the best way for a property owner to connect with you and your team and send us off in the right direction to come up with a strategy?

Richard

The best way to contact us is at **www.Richardhollowell.com**. I can make my senior consultants available by phone and actually a couple of them have been court-appointed receivers and/or easing specialists themselves. We're happy to have a short consultation to see if we can help the situation.

11.

I own a retail strip center, what should I be thinking about as I fear that all my tenants will not reopen due to COVID?

Andy

Andy Broadaway here and I'm with Richard Hollowell. And this is a continuing series of interview questions on how commercial real estate is being affected by COVID. The question I have for you that came in from someone that visited your website is, "I own a retail strip center, what should I be thinking about as I fear that all of my local tenants will not reopen due to the COVID?

Richard

Andy, you have to feel for retail property owners because the COVID shutdown has been really tough for small tenants; one-half of those tenants that are not banks, pharmacies, grocery stores, or home improvement stores didn't pay rent in April. It will be worse for the May to August period. We have new statistics coming in each day. Some of our local retail stores re-opened here in mid-June in my neighborhood, and as I drove through those centers during the last week of June, there were few people in the stores or cars in the parking lots. From my perspective, the retail property owner has to manage two things.

Number one, work with tenants to get them open and try to get them paying some level of rent, and work with them in hopes of keeping them in place until the holiday season when they may return to paying full rent. Second, you have to start working immediately with your lender to come up with a forbearance program that will give you time to work with each and every tenant, and then come up with a concrete plan you can take to your lender based on your discussions every tenant. You have to focus every day on taking steps to rebuild your cash flow.

Retail property owners are up against some tough odds here because lenders are smart and they're looking at all the statistical data for the retail industry issued by the rating agencies and major retail brokers. Today, the data shows that of the top 100 restaurant and retail businesses in the country 15% have a high chance of failing in the months to come. It will be much worse than that for smaller, non-national tenants where up to 40% might fail. So, the retail property owner has to try to keep these tenants in place on some kind of basis, because the worst case is the tenant vacates and you have an empty space with no takers.

You simply don't want to have to replace small tenants if you can help it for the next 12 months, because replacing tenants will cost you leasing commissions, the cost of tenant finishes and perhaps free rent or other concessions, and that's if you're lucky enough to find a tenant. That's your major challenge until there is some certainty about the direction of COVID.

The extra cost of replacing tenants may simply be too high once you pencil out those expenses and time frames, especially in a market that is void of tenant prospects. So, I'm recommending that you be as proactive as you can to secure a payment arrangement with each tenant, then coming up with a solid plan that you think is salable to your lender.

Andy

I totally agree. I'm driving by retail outlets and I'm seeing some of the stores open back up again, but I'm also looking at the mall itself and only the big retail outlets are open, few of the smaller stores are open. So, Richard, you're recommending to be very proactive in coming up with individual tenant strategies, right?

Richard

Absolutely, you've got to be as proactive as you can; your individual tenant strategies will set the stage for your discussion with your lender. This discussion takes me back to my past receiverships when I would take over a troubled property under the direction of a court. The properties were in foreclosure; I would walk into a situation where multiple tenants were in default. Sometimes they would try to gang-up on you as the receiver and march into your office all together asking for each to receive a rent reduction. On one occasion there was even a "rent strike" by all tenants when I was running a large Florida mall as a receiver. So, you have to be as proactive as you can to keep tenants pacified, and paying some level of rent, particularly as you work to get your property's income stream ramped up as soon as practicable.

Andy

Ideally, I suppose you want it to be a win, win situation. As the owner, you need to keep tenants in place to generate foot traffic which results in sales; with no sales, tenants can't pay rent. I guess it's all about foot traffic and shoppers. At the same time, you've got to come up with a strategy for the lender.

Richard

That's correct, and you never want to underestimate the retail or market knowledge that your lender has. Believe me, the lender is keeping up with what's going on in the retail world. Remember, your lender knows that online shopping on the websites of the top-10 retailers will double in just the next three years. And that will have a further negative affect on brick and mortar centers. So, they are watching the changing dynamics of retail, they know that in a normal year 10,000 retail stores may close, but because of COVID, they also know that experts say 50,000 stores will close in the next 12 months. So, you need to dig deep into the financial future of all your tenants and proactively come up with a realistic view of your future income stream. Get your documentation in order as your lender will certainly challenge you.

Andy

So as a follow up question to that, as the owner of a shopping center, what financing or refinancing options do I have when talking to my lender?

Richard

Your current lender is likely the only lender available to you now. Why, because if you are experiencing reduced cash flow you've got to deal with the lender. What you'll be seeking is a loan modification or a loan extension to get you past this COVID downturn and the uncertainty of the market. So, you better have a well-documented, solid plan, and probably some additional money available to offer the deal in order to persuade the lender that a loan workout is the best course. Generally, you can't ask for an interest rate cut, a partial payment plan, or accrual of payments without exchange of value such as some new investment. Just remember, don't alienate your lender, because it's my opinion that he's the only lender you may have for a while.

Andy

And that makes sense. So, is that something that you and your team can help a property owner with, coming up with a well-documented strategy, then presenting it to the lender? Is that something that your company does?

Richard

That's what we do, we've developed dozens, if not hundreds of restructuring plans for different types of real estate over the years. And, we know what's in the lender's playbook, we know exactly what they're looking for when you walk in, and when we put together a presentation, it will be in a format that is almost ready to be adopted by the lender's workout specialist to present to the loan committee for approval. Basically, we perform the lenders' due diligence and other homework for them to shortcut the process and the time required to get a loan forbearance or a modification in place. Our team is very skilled at managing the process.

Andy

What I like about your team is that you have worked on both sides of the playing field in the past; sometimes helping the lender, and sometimes helping borrowers.

Richard

Andy, my group excels in working on both sides of the equation. We've worked for banks, we've been bankers, we've been CMBS special servicers, but more so we've worked for the borrowers that need a liaison with the lender so that the client's plan can get the attention it deserves. Every one of our Senior Consultants has the skills that are requisite to put together a presentation that's effectively loan committee ready. Folks can get more information about our people and about the things that we do at **www.Richardhollowell.com.**

12.

As a retail mall owner, what advice would you give me when dealing with my current tenants?

Andy

Andy Broadaway here and I'm with Richard and I'm asking him a series of real estate related questions. So, if your question isn't being answered in this particular interview, you may find it in one of the other interviews. My question to you today is, "Richard, many describe what is going on right now as the COVID virus retail apocalypse. What is your specific strategy of hope for retail property owners?"

Richard

Well, my wife has told me for the last 20 years, especially as we went through the great recession and a big real estate downturn from 2008 to 2012, "Richard, you can't go around being Dr. Doom, you've got to give people hope and tell them how to manage their problems." So, she's actually a great leader in her own business and possesses a lot of wisdom. The first thing I would likely tell to retail owners is they need to hold lengthy, detailed meetings with each and every one of their tenants. They need to take a look at what the tenant's performance was for 2019, then put together some going forward projections with each tenant, all with the goal of keeping the tenant in place, while maximizing short-term and long-term rent collections.

I think retail centers are going to be one of the toughest property types to bring back from COVID. As stores re-open and shoppers feel safe to go back into shops, I think the level at which bricks and mortar will recover will come down to Black Friday. That's less than 90 days away and will tell us a lot about the prospects for industry recovery. So today, I would focus on fully understanding the operations of each tenant, the seasonal nature of their businesses, and then determine their potential cash flow and a realistic rent payment schedule. Next, I would also be thinking about repositioning the center and consider alternative uses for vacant space, which may include altering a distinct area of the retail center into a non-retail use. If you think you're going to have significant scattered vacancies, consider moving your best tenants to a specific area in the center so as to then reposition contiguous vacant space.

Andy

That's an interesting thought, so how do you determine how to use that chunk of vacant space?

Richard

I think you start by analyzing what's going on in your market. I'd be asking myself what demand drivers exist for the area, have area demographics changed, what the potential uses for vacant space are and which alternatives would generate the highest rents, at what cost. One national retail developer who owns a huge retail portfolio has done just that. They're actually going to demolish a portion of their retail center and use the vacant land to build a four-story apartment. I saw schematics on that very plan and the concept looked great.

And when you talk about vacant department stores, because you know, Neiman Marcus, JC Penny and Lord and Taylor have filed bankruptcy, plus Macy's is closing stores, while Nordstrom announced that they can't pay more than ½ their rent until 2021, an owner must get creative. A top feasibility expert can help assess the alternatives, then put together financial projections for each use. So, I see folks talking about putting fulfillment centers in vacant department store spaces, or converting department stores to apartment or loft concept residential uses.

It will be interesting, but you're going to have to evaluate as many re-use scenarios as possible. Earlier in my career, we actually converted a historic City Hall to office space, then master leased the building to a power company. We also took a historic, abandoned train station and created office and retail space, and then converted nine five-story bottling warehouses into a three-story outlet mall and two stories of office space. Owners should be creative and embrace a spirit of hope and optimism for recovery. We will be pleased to provide some coaching and engender creative thinking in their process.

Andy

Well, that's a great answer. Um, you know, when you say Dr. Gloom and Doom, I actually didn't even think of you that way because I go back to reading an article and I'm not sure where it was published, but the title of the article was "The Fixer". And so, I see you as being a property and loan fixer.

For those people that don't know about that article, give us some color on how you were nicknamed "The Fixer."

Richard

Well, it's interesting. I didn't actually come up with that title. It actually was made up by a business reporter at the Orange County register who wrote that article in November of 2007; that was right before the real estate collapse that started in 2008. The article discusses how I assist developers who have defaulted on loans with their banks and oftentimes get their loans restructured, and/or their personal guarantees released. This was similar to an earlier article back in 2002 after the 911 attack when I was restructuring troubled aviation companies in Miami. That article was entitled "Befriending your lender in troubled times." So that article was written to give aviation operators some hope, suggesting methods to persuade your lender to modify a troubled loan.

Andy

I really like your approach, Richard, because your approach is let's get all the facts, let's put them together and then let me have my teams strategically come up with a presentation, a package with a proforma that we can present to a lender to try to gain some financial concessions. I remember a quote that Tony Robbins makes, he says, see things as they are not bigger than they are. And I think that's the approach that you really give to your clients is allowing them to see things as they are not bigger than what they are. Am I correct?

Richard

You're correct there, Andy, it's our job to make an independent analysis that is well documented, resulting in a proposal that is saleable to a lender. Sometimes we have to deliver bad news to our clients, telling them the reasons that "their" workout proposals won't work. We never deliver a pie in the sky" projections to a lender, because they're going to see right through it. Remember, we've sat on the lender's side of the desk so we know their analytical methods, how they'll conduct their due diligence, and what and how they have to present credit decisions on problem loans to internal credit decision makers. So, we are able to see all facets of a potential loan from both perspectives of the borrower and the lender. I believe that is probably the greatest value we can add to the situation.

Andy

Wonderful. So where could we find out more information about potentially working with you and your team and what does the process look like?

Richard

Well, you can go to **www.Richardhollowell.com** on our website. You can take a look at all of our qualifications, the credentials of our team members, and right on the front page, there's a form that you can populate that says, let us know about your conflict, and from that we'll set up an initial consultation. We'll see if we think it's the type of thing that we can help with. So, folks that want to reach us can go to **www.Richardhollowell.com**.

13.

As an office building owner, how do I expect the work-from-home requirements that exist during COVID to affect my ability to lease vacant space and get terminating leases renewed?

Andy

Andy Broadaway here and I'm back with another question for Richard. And as you know, this is a continuing series about the negative effects the COVID shutdown is having on commercial real estate. This series includes the answers to 17 key questions real estate owners are asking in these very troubled times. So today Richard, my question to you is, "As an office building owner, how will work-from-home requirements that exist during COVID affect my ability to lease vacant space and get expiring leases renewed?"

Richard

That's an issue that really hits home, Andy. I'm actually monitoring the performance of a huge office building partnership on behalf of limited partners whose investments facilitated over $500 million of office building purchases. So, I'm watching the effects of COVID on this portfolio day in and day out. The office owner really has two key challenges right now. Let's remember that office buildings are rarely 100% leased. So, today you have the vacant space challenge, first, getting people to come and look at available space in your building, and second, you may have expiring leases to renew. And we could sit here and talk for two hours about this subject because I've compiled and synthesized a wealth of information on a national basis, but we'll try to break it down into a couple of short answers. For starters, you will have better success leasing vacant space in the suburbs as opposed to the central business district.

The reason is there are many companies at this point that are looking to re-locate from the central business district because of the dense business population in the CBD, crowded elevators, and public transit problems. Thus, many would-be CBD tenants are now opting for locations in the suburbs. That's issue number one to keep an eye on. If you're a CBD office building owner, you better be working closely with your tenants. In doing so, you'll need to hone in on which tenants are and which ones are not truly affected by COVID. I've seen firms that have not missed a beat in their earning power during the work-from-home period ask for and actually receive rent reduction packages. As an owner, it's a mistake to give rent abatement or rent forgiveness, because in my book you never forgive anything.

As an owner, you want to include a mechanism to get back any rent you're not collecting now, at some point in the near future. I know here in Los Angeles, a very large firm that I'm familiar with a 60,000 square foot lease will not have its employees return to their space until sometime after Labor Day, and maybe not until January 2021. And I don't think that this is an isolated observation. In my city, where there are plenty of 10-15 story office buildings, I still see very few cars in the parking lots and we are now in August 2020.

I see companies that are seriously considering downsizing because they realized that during the whole work-from-home scenario, work productivity has not been significantly affected, if at all. Executives and staff simply pick up their computers, sit in a home office or at a kitchen table, and work gets done. And in this digital era where technology is so advanced, why spend two hours in a commute as opposed to sitting at your kitchen table? The only question I have is how will management effectively provide oversight to employees, and how, for example, do you motivate people who might have a dog distracting them at their feet all day. With those things considered, as a company's lease approaches renewal, they will carefully analyze how much office space they really need. In both suburban and the CBD settings, tenants that have completed this analysis over the last 30 days have found that they can run their businesses effectively with 20% to 25% less space.

A tenant may review its lease and will likely find that there is a subleasing clause, which may allow the tenant to sublease a portion of their space. Depending on the clause's terms for landlord approval, leasing competition with the building's owner could result, which may end up adversely impacting the landlord/tenant relationship. As a court-appointed receiver for office buildings, I often ended up competing with my current tenants who wanted to sublease space. And, of course, in many cases, you cannot unreasonably withhold approval of a request. And it becomes a bigger problem when your own tenant seeks to sublease a portion of its space at what otherwise is below market; word of that gets out in the leasing community. So again, it's a very sensitive issue that in some way could impact your cash flow.

Another dynamic caused by the COVID shutdown are increasing liability insurance costs and enhanced cleaning protocols which must be put in place to sanitize the entire office building environment. As an office building owner who faces lease expirations in the coming 6-9 months, I suggest that you proactively meet with tenants, so you are not blind-sided by a move-out, down-size, or sublease situation that causes you a problem. And remember, your lender is ramping up surveillance. You must also be cognizant of loan provisions that require lender approval rights on major leases. I highly recommend that an owner stay ahead of your lender in focusing on lease renewals.

Andy

So how specifically can you and your team help out a commercial property owner to best communicate, not just with tenants, but also communicate with lenders?

Richard

One of the things that we bring to the table is that we look at damaged borrower cash flows and tenant move-outs from the lenders perspective; remember, we've worked on a couple of thousand loan defaults from the lender's side of the equation, and your lender will be analyzing the financial condition of your property as it surveils for loan covenant defaults. Many lenders require you to submit quarterly rent rolls, and financial results and forecasts of future cash flow on a periodic basis. Where we can help is to assist in taking a realistic look at your situation, prepare a go-forward operating and leasing strategy, then package a request that we'll present to the lender on the borrower's behalf as part of any workout request for a forbearance or loan modification.

Andy

Well, that's awesome. So how can we get more information? Where do we go to speak with you and your team?

Richard

Folks can take a look at our website, which is **www.Richardhollowell.com**. Once there, they can look at our qualifications in this particular area under a tab called real estate solutions. Again, the website is **www.Richardhollowell**.com.

14.

Some describe what is going on as the coronavirus retail apocalypse, what is your strategy of hope?

Andy

Andy Broadaway here and again, I'm with Richard Hollowell and this is a series of interviews and questions regarding commercial real estate, hospitality, retail space, et cetera. So, Richard, I know that nobody has their crystal ball, because if they did, we would have known that the Pandemic was going to occur, and we could have prepared for it. However, in your opinion, where do you see things pivoting?

Richard

Well, you're correct, that is a crystal ball question. And it's interesting, in 2008 when I was asked to give predictions before public audiences, I actually bought a crystal ball and set it on the podium as a prop. And of course, everybody's heard the word pivoting over and over, especially on CNBC. What you've given me Andy are several questions boiled into one.

Let's start with retail shopping centers because that's the asset class that was being adversely affected by on-line shopping before the Covid Pandemic. Let's be honest, people have gotten used to buying goods online, and the Pandemic has drawn even more people to online shopping. Frankly, people of all ages now enjoy the online shopping experience. Even when shopping centers open across the board, it's my prediction that foot traffic will be down for quite a while, and less foot traffic means lower sales, and lower sales mean that tenants can't pay the rent they previously agreed to pay. Hence, evictions, move-outs, and/or tenant bankruptcies. Add to the equation predictions that in two years online retail sales will grow by 30%, while 60% of ALL global commerce will be transacted digitally, so the only way retail centers will survive is to reposition the property for other uses. The land around major shopping centers is vast, which is now used for parking to a great extent. So, I think you'll see portions of a retail center demolished in favor of say, apartments or medical office uses, or unused out parcels slated for similar developments.

Commercial real estate, especially retail centers, hotels, and office buildings will flounder in my opinion until an effective, preventative vaccine is found and administered to get to herd immunity. I don't see that happening until the end of 2021. I stand by my thoughts that the multifamily and industrial asset classes will continue to do well, excepting perhaps multifamily in city centers where residents have started to exit for the suburbs.

Simply, people need a place to live, and commerce flows through industrial/warehouse properties. These are not asset classes that rely on the digital world to a great extent.

Now comes office space which in my opinion will be changed forever by the work-at-home mandate of COVID. There is no question in my mind that corporate office users will downsize their space in the months and years to come. I see people going to the office in shifts, maybe switching in-office desks with their colleagues every two weeks. With technology as efficient as it is today, and technology expanding productivity at light speed, business will continue uninterrupted, and businesses will prosper with 20% to 25% less office space. Here's a bit of a parallel, I was running a large company in the early 1990's when "Casual Friday" became fashionable. I wasn't crazy about the whole concept as I came from a three-piece suit environment, and I watched "Casual Friday" become "Sloppy Friday." My perspective was that the concept would never stick, but I was proven very wrong. Today, business gets done and people are sitting at home in workout clothes all day!

Then on to suburban offices which will again be fashionable as employers will be looking to keep their employees safe from mass transit, busy pedestrian traffic, and cramped elevators. Also challenging for the office building owner will be the subleasing of space which is brought about by downsizing. So, three years from now, you should see a whole new picture of the way offices are leased, and of course used by tenants. Technology and its rapid advances will change the face of office demand.

So, the so-called "pivot comes only when a COVID vaccine is found and administered to the masses. So, I'm not a doctor, and have no medical training, although our daughter is a highly-skilled physician. What I do know after many, many years is that people are in a state of concern if not apprehension. No one has experienced a contagious pandemic, and people are shell shocked by the prospect of coming in contact with people. When I walk my dog along the sidewalk and another dog owner approaches, they will veer to the other side of the street 60 feet away! And I have close friends who we would meet for dinner every Friday evening, and they've told us not to expect them until a vaccine is developed and proven effective. To me, there is nothing short of a vaccine that will convince anyone over age 40 to go back to "business as usual"

Andy

Yeah. I totally agree with you that I think people in general, they need to have some certainty knowing that when they go somewhere, they're going to be safe. People are having a lot of difficulty right now dealing with uncertainty. And so, how can your team offer hope to commercial real estate owners in the retail, hotel and office industries?

Richard

Andy, we try to address their cash flow challenge and the repositioning of their properties with an eye to rebuilding their cash flow under the watchful eye of their lender. Lenders will be under incredible stress for the next 18 months so our goal for the client is to develop workout solutions that the lender representative can sell to their loan committees because we've all been members of those loan committees. We know what works and won't work. We know how to develop projections that are realistic and well documented, and we know how to deliver those proposals better than the typical borrower/owner does.

For those that want to go after their lender on their own, we'll be straight and tell you why you'll succeed, or be shot down. So, I think that's really where we add value.

Andy

Wonderful. How do we reach you? And what's the best way to communicate with you and your team?

Richard:

The best way to communicate with us is to go to our website, which is **www.Richardhollowell.com**. On the landing page, one will see a form that can be populated to briefly describe their challenge. You can be specific, telling us about the problem they have with their property, their tenants, or their lender. It's a confidential submission of facts that will give us a foundation for an initial conversation. A problem I've seen over the last 40 years is that borrowers wait in a state of denial too long, then we get a call too late after the lender has taken drastic steps to enforce its rights. So, we encourage borrowers to call us early, so we can extend a lifeline of sorts, and perhaps hold their lender at bay. So, we encourage folks to go to **www.Richardhollowell.com** where they can populate the form discussed above and we can set up an initial consultation.

15.

Do I dare ask you where you think hotel owners will land due to COVID?

Andy

Andy Broadaway and I'm with Richard Hollowell at **Richardhollowell.com**. And this is a series of interviews across the board involving the way commercial real estate is being affected by the COVID shutdown. And if you haven't listened to the other interviews, go back because I'm sure that the question you have will be answered in one of our previous interviews. So, Richard, my question to you is, "Do I really dare ask, where do you think hotel owners will land given the hotel industry shutdown caused by Covid-19?"

Richard

Hospitality is the most damaged real estate asset class out there right now because occupancies literally went to zero overnight. We have a major luxury hotel right in our own backyard, it's about 500 rooms, and the word is that the hotel will not reopen until early 2021. And, here's what I'm hearing on the street after talking to a lot of folks that are actually assembling money to buy distressed hotel properties. What I'm hearing on the street is that 35% of the value is gone from a hotel property today, at least temporarily, and 20% of hotel loans were in default as of May 1st. And when hotels finally reopen, they're going to be at much lower occupancies with increased expenses due to the cost of continuously cleaning rooms and common areas, and the recent spike in insurance costs. Owners will have to continuously assure their guests that their establishment is Covid-free.

Now, another thing that has started in some hotels is that guests checking into a hotel are being required to sign a liability release should the guest contract Covid during their stay. In essence, a guest contracting Covid has to give up their rights to litigation if they want to spend the night at certain hotels. Personally, I haven't been to a hotel since COVID, yet we frequent hotels all over the country. Our first experience at a hotel post-Covid will be in late July, so we'll see how that goes. So here is an interesting first hand story, I have a former client that actually has four very nice, branded airport hotels, all shut down because of Covid. They were able to approach the master servicer for their CMBS loan and get a 90-day forbearance on payments beginning on April 1st due to the shutdown.

My client was <u>not</u> a bit alarmed that his forbearance period would run out July 31st, and he fully expects to approach the CMBS Special Servicer and obtain an acceptable loan modification. I guarantee that he has no idea how his Special Servicer will treat his request. I know the behavior patterns of CMBS lenders and I know exactly how they'll approach his situation. With business travel still down over 75%, there is no way he can show his lender even 50% occupancy, a level that will not support his debt service payments, and the hotels' Average Daily Rate (ADR) will also be negatively affected. A high-level industry insider tells me that neither hotel occupancies nor ADR's will return to 2019 levels until at least 2024. That assumes there's some kind of Covid vaccine in 2021 that will help folks return to a mindset where they feel comfortable going to a hotel to the same degree as before. Believe me, a hotel lender's patience will run out by the fall of 2020 and cash infusion from the borrower will be required to orchestrate a loan modification. Simply, non-earning assets don't look good on anybody's books. Many lenders will just step in, put a court appointed receiver in place, take over the property and sell it to one of many vulture funds who have already assembled the money to buy troubled hotels.

Andy

Thanks for that answer. And I recall you saying in another interview that lenders do not want to be in the real estate business, they just want to be in the business of lending money. So, the last thing they want to do is foreclose and step into the owner's shoes, but sometimes it's unavoidable. So, is it best to hire someone like yourself to get a head start on dealing with the lender?

Richard

That often helps Andy. One thing folks need to think about in the hospitality industry is how much additional money they can invest in their property because loan modifications won't come easy. Lenders don't want non-earning assets, and they'll come after you if you don't proactively approach them, identify problems and providing solutions through a feasible workout plan. That's a process we can help with and we are very good at delivering a plan to a lender as the advocate of the borrower. Remember, we know the mindset of the lender and the rules he's playing by, so folks can reach us at **www.Richardhollowell.com** and we can talk about hotel financing challenges.

16.

With some anchor retail tenants posed to go dark or terminate their leases in a bankruptcy, how do I evaluate the co-tenancy provision in my lease?

Andy

Andy Broadaway here and I'm here with Richard Hollowell. In prior interviews, we've asked a series of questions involving how the Covid shutdown is affecting the commercial real estate industry. Today's subject involves the bankruptcy of large department stores, and how that affects smaller local tenants. I have a local tenant asking, "How do I evaluate the co-tenancy provisions in my lease?"

Richard

Andy, that's a question that I'm getting from tenants who occupy between 2,500 to 25,000 square feet in large shopping centers anchored by department stores. These are tenants that rely on the foot traffic generated by a department store. What a typical co-tenancy provision says is that if a given department store stops operating, a smaller tenant may opt-out of their lease. Examples of troubled department stores are Neiman Marcus, J.C. Penney, and Lord & Taylor all of which are in bankruptcy. And outside of bankruptcy, you have department stores like Macy's who have announced the closing of some 155 stores. If those stores close and go dark, the shopping center is not creating the foot-traffic that you expected as a smaller tenant. The benefit of a co-tenancy clause is that it would allow you to vacate your space without incurring any liability. It can also provide the smaller tenant with leverage if the tenant would prefer to stay in place and negotiate a rent reduction, which the landlord may prefer.

Retail tenants will want to look to see if they have a co-tenancy provision in their lease. As a critical term in a lease, a sophisticated tenant will know if they have co-tenancy rights. Many less sophisticated tenants who don't know to negotiate this into their leases usually won't find this provision.

On the other hand, if you're the property owner, you better know if this provision is in your leases as you may have a major problem should one of your major tenants close a store or file bankruptcy. In essence, if a department store goes dark, a number of smaller tenants might leave right behind.

Andy

So, Richard, if I'm either a property owner or a smaller tenant, what is the best way to communicate to you? And when should we call you?

Richard

Well, if there's a challenge in analyzing co-tenancy clauses or other clauses in the lease, we can be contacted at **www.Richardhollowell.com.** Most property owners know whether or not they have co-tenancy exposure. Now on the tenant side, we typically work with tenants that occupy 5,000 square feet and above. Those are of the size where they may have a co-tenancy clause that we can analyze and help determine the merits and likelihood for obtaining a rent abatement, a lowering of your total rent or a component of it. We can also analyze the factors that might lead you to decide whether to vacate that space or not. Tenants who have such issues tenants can reach out to us at **www.Richardhollowell.com** for a consultation.

17.

I Own an Upscale Shopping Center and I Have Several Restaurant Tenants, both In-Line and on Out-Parcels; Their Revenue has been Devastated By COVID, What are My Alternatives if They Go Dark?

Andy

Andy Broadaway here and I'm conversing with Richard Hollowell about the way real estate owners and their tenants are being affected by the COVID Pandemic. You'll recall that Richard has worn many hats over five decades including as developer, broker, financial intermediary, property manager, court appointed receiver, banker, CMBS special servicer, and expert witness. Our question today Richard comes from an upscale shopping center owner who asks, "I own an Upscale Shopping Center and I have several restaurant tenants, both In-Line and on Out-Parcels; their revenue has been devastated by COVID, what are my alternatives if they go dark?"

Richard

Before I get to your question Andy, I think we should first discuss just how crippled the restaurant industry is due to COVID. According to the National Restaurant Association, restaurants lost $120 billion this year through May and, collectively, restaurants are expected to lose $240 billion by year end. In April, more than 8 million restaurant employees were unemployed.

Here are the reasons why I so appreciate restaurant owners; just consider the risks of being in the restaurant business, which innately include (i) theft, (ii) equipment costs, (iii) food safety, (iv) cleanliness, (v) liquor liability, (vi) fire safety, (vii) staff turnover, (viii) shifting food tastes, and (ix) injuries, among others. Then add across the board restaurant shutdown due to a Global Pandemic and it's no wonder experts have said that up to 230,000 restaurants might permanently close by the end of this year.

Can you imagine the pressure a restaurant owner is under knowing that for every dollar that comes in, between 90 and 95 cents goes out the door; in normal times it's a slim margin business for most operators. Then, couple these statistics with the fact that a dozen nationally recognized restaurants have already filed bankruptcy with more are on the way in the weeks and months to come.

Here's an "off the record" quote from a successful Southern California white table cloth restaurateur, "We absolutely can't survive at 50% occupancy." Then, an on-the-record quote I heard on CBS Sunday Morning from Danny Meyer, Founder and CEO of Union Square Hospitality Group in New York City, "We have 20 restaurants in New York City and they are all closed, break-even starts at 80% occupancy. To me, the combined impact of these quotes is absolutely chilling as I regard these owners to be among the finest in the country.

Andy

Boiled together, everything you've told me so far is quite depressing, so if I'm a property owner and a landlord to one or more of these restaurants, what do I do? My lender is clamoring for his mortgage payment and he's not giving me much time to come up with a plan, so what do I do first?

Richard

As someone who has negotiated unsubordinated ground leases with national restaurant companies, and managed large shopping centers as a court appointed receiver, I can sympathize with restaurateurs. First, you must focus on completing an analysis of how each restaurant tenant has been truly impacted. If I'm your lender, I'm expecting you to know the sales volume of each restaurant in 2019. Then, I want a monthly analysis of your restaurant tenant's business, starting with their new hours of operation, how much ownership is taking out of the operation, what is dropping to the bottom line, and how the bottom line, if any is distributed. Another big point, you want to know about and track is all non-operational cash coming into the business, including PPP money provided by the government to support employee payroll payments; that's a non-operational inflow of revenue that needs to be removed from recurring revenue to truly determine current operating results. And make sure your tenant is judiciously using its PPP money and following government guideline; and why, I just saw an announcement on August 21st from a major accounting firm that alerted their clients to upcoming PPP audits by the government. If I'm your lender, I want to be absolutely sure my borrowers are following PPP guidelines.

From the perspective of the owner, I do not automatically forgive rent; yet, until COVID is controlled, I may waive today's fixed rent in favor of a percentage rent based on gross sales numbers. Depending on the type of restaurant, the percentage may vary by a few percentage points plus or minus. I may then require that any missed payments (arrearage) and any accumulated deficit (being the difference between the new percentage rent and the original fixed rent), be placed on a negotiated repayment, starting after the effects of Pandemic are effectively over. In some cases, consider requiring additional collateral from your restauranteur or other credit enhancements such as additional guarantees to secure the payment plan. But you have to understand at what point not to overreach in your demands because your tenant may find a bankruptcy judge more friendly in giving the financial relief that you won't.

Andy

Wow, knowing when to stop pushing sounds like a major challenge that is full of risk. What do you see happening in the industry as Summer ends and we get into the Fall season?

Richard

Landlords should keep a close eye on what the newly formed Independent Restaurant Coalition is doing. Currently, they are lobbying Congress for $120 billion of bailout money to support restaurants through the end of 2020, which may enable restaurateurs to pay more of their rent than they are currently paying from operations. You also need to monitor the legislation being lobbied by the Commercial Real Estate Finance Council (CREFC) on behalf of the special servicing industry. That legislation, if passed, would provide more than $400 billion of subsidies to CMBS lenders. That financial support may pave an easier path for a borrower to obtain longer term forbearances and less onerous loan modifications. We are watching both of these issues closely. In the end, I encourage property owners to remember one thing, do everything possible to keep your restaurant tenants alive, because replacing a restaurant tenant for the next 12 months will be near impossible.

Andy

So Richard, It sounds like you're on top of all the movement in the restaurant industry, how does someone reach you if they would like to enlist your guidance?

Richard

Folks can go to our website Andy at **www.Richardhollowell.com.** Once there, you'll find a short form to fill out where you can explain your challenge and we can set up an initial phone consultation. Simply look up our website at **www.Richardhollowell.com.**

Testimonials

"Our company was heavily invested in a South Florida real estate redevelopment deal when the bubble burst in 2008 and values quickly plummeted. Our lender failed, sold our personally-guaranteed note to an individual investor, and we were faced with a problem unlike any that we had previously encountered despite having successfully navigated a $500MM workout during the 1990-91 recession.

Even with our prior experience, it was Richard Hollowell's comprehensive evaluation of all portfolio assets and preparation of supporting materials that presented a compelling summary of the borrower's financial status and enabled our creditor to cooperate with us on a substantially-discounted plan.

This approach, implemented in 2009, worked for us and in retrospect would not have been possible without Richard's outstanding effort, perfect communication, and high-level guidance. Having worked with a major retail developer for more than thirty years, it is clear that our collaborating with Richard at such a vulnerable time was one of the most significant successes that we have experienced relative to the enormity of the challenge before us."

Scott D. Hornaday
President
David Hocker Associates
Owensboro, KY

"Richard Hollowell is a true professional, who brings tremendous in-depth personal knowledge and perspective in evaluating and addressing complex distressed commercial real estate situations – a person who has actually been there, done that, not a pontificator.

A little over a year ago while representing a national restaurant chain in litigation with one of the nation's largest owners of retail malls, I was fortunate to work with Richard as an expert consultant and trial witness.

Demonstrating a genuine ability to distill complicated statistical analysis and financial information and explain it in a way that is easy to understand, Richard artfully presented his opinions with compelling professionalism and was at the center of the trial verdict in favor of our client."

William F. Ryan Jr.
Partner, Litigation Practice Co-Chair
Whiteford Taylor Preston
www.wtplaw.com
Baltimore, MD

"My partner John George and I retained Richard Hollowell to assist us in litigation brought by the Federal Deposit Insurance Corporation as receiver of one of the largest community banks to fail in Illinois during the Great Recession. The FDIC sued the bank's former officers and directors to recover several hundred million dollars in alleged losses on dozens of commercial loans to borrowers in the hospitality industry in Illinois, New York, and Florida.

Richard's unique expertise in banking and the relevant commercial real estate markets and his experience as a testifying witness provided invaluable assistance in responding to the FDIC's allegations about supposed lending deficiencies as well as the claimed damages.

It was a professional and personal pleasure to work with someone as talented and knowledgeable as Richard and we look forward to opportunities to do so again in the future."

Nancy A. Temple
Partner
Katten & Temple LLP
www.kattentemple.com
Chicago, IL

"I've had the pleasure of knowing Richard Hollowell for over 30 years; during that time I have dealt with him in my role as an attorney in my legal practice. I have consistently witnessed his ability to create effective workout strategies, in both complex and relatively straightforward distressed real estate situations, and then to execute competently and efficiently thereby maximizing the value of the asset. He also demonstrated excellent communication skills which was very important to me.

I've also dealt with Richard in my former role as the Chairman of a Florida based community bank with the same type of admiration for the services he provided.

I have the utmost confidence in not only Richard's skill, acumen and ability as a professional, but also, and perhaps more importantly, in his rock-solid integrity."

Brian Sherr
Shareholder
Greenberg Traurig, LLP
www.gtlaw.com
Ft. Lauderdale, FL

"In the aftermath of the Great Recession, Richard Hollowell assisted one of my clients in a complicated litigation and ultimate successful work-out. The financings involved two banks and the resolution of, among other things, real estate and other pledged asset valuations.

Richard, who was a pleasure to work with and added significant credibility to our position, served as the client's banking expert and testified as to best practices in the banking industry for underwriting and approving real estate financings."

Les Jacobowitz
Partner
Arent Fox LLP
www.arentfox.com
New York, NY

"I have had the absolute pleasure of knowing Richard Hollowell for close to 20 years, initially meeting through a mutual colleague regarding a Las Vegas casino redevelopment project on the Las Vegas Strip. What I learned then and what has been reinforced time and again since is there are few real estate experts with the breadth of knowledge and experience that Richard possesses.

As we head into an unprecedented time of headwinds in the commercial real estate industry, his experience will be needed more than ever. And even more importantly, Richard is a person of integrity and honesty - qualities more important than any item on his long and accomplished resume!"

Stephen A. Crystal
Head of North America Development
Betfred USA Sports
Las Vegas, NV

"I have known Richard Hollowell for over 30 years. During that time I witnessed his ability to resolve complex distressed commercial real estate assets with creativity and determination, always the consummate professional. During the early stages of the Resolution Trust Corporation (RTC) my firm, Real Estate Recovery, Inc., was awarded one of the largest SAMDA contracts, charged with the orderly disposition of defaulted real estate loans.

Richard, as Executive Vice President, was assigned the responsibility of establishing our Florida office, which under his leadership, grew to become the largest of our six regional offices, and a constant recipient of additional work from the government based upon the track record he developed.

Then as President of the firm with a staff expanded to 175 professionals, he evaluated, developed exit strategies, litigated, restructured and disposed of over $1 billion of real estate assets. Throughout this period, Richard's integrity and interpersonal skills combined to make him a most sought-after professional by our bank and government agency financial clients. After the sunset of the RTC, Richard formed his own firm with which we collaborated on a number of major projects including portfolio acquisitions, debt restructurings and distressed bank consulting. Richard is truly one of the most knowledgeable and experienced workout specialists in the country."

Christopher Kallivokas
Manager
RER Ventures LLC
Coral Gables, FL

"Richard is one of the premier real estate experts in the nation. With experience handling a wide range of real estate projects both from a development and workout perspective, Richard brings a unique perspective to every real estate matter. In my previous complex real estate litigation practice, I often called upon Richard to serve as an expert witness.

I was amazed with his ability to quickly digest complex real estate issues and then communicate those issues in a way that could be easily understood by both the lawyers and the triers of fact.

There are not many real estate experts with Richard's breadth of experience and I enthusiastically recommend Richard as a real estate consultant and expert witness."

Alan S. Petlak
Petlak Mediation
www.petlakmediation.com
Los Angeles, CA

"As we find ourselves approaching what may be a major downturn in commercial real estate markets, distressed property and note investors are poised to capitalize on significant opportunities. Richard Hollowell is one of a select few 'godfathers' of distressed real estate investing and financial restructurings.

Richard advised us on a 1,600 bed student housing property restructuring in the 2015-2016 period and demonstrated the depth of his experience and expertise. Richard's ability to engage constructively with lenders and special servicers, to think strategically about 'win-win' outcomes for both the borrower and lender, and to anticipate questions and incorporate those answers into presentation materials are priceless."

Mitch Siegler
Senior Managing Director and Co-Founder
Pathfinder Partners
www.pathfinderfunds.com
San Diego, CA

"Richard Hollowell assisted our firm as a testifying expert in the defense of a general partner in a lawsuit involving a Southern California waterfront shopping village. His knowledge of available financing in the 2008-2010 time period, coupled with his experience in unsubordinated ground leases allowed us to successfully defend the general partner, after which the judge awarded our client all legal fees and expert witness costs.

I would wholeheartedly recommend Richard as a professional who is equipped to deliver solutions in hard to defend real estate disputes."

Michael Lyon
Partner
Procopio, Cory, Hargreaves & Savitch, LLP
www.procopio.com
San Diego, CA

"I have had the privilege of working with Richard Hollowell for several years. I have recommended him as an expert witness and his guidance and expertise have always been appreciated.

I look to him for advice on highly technical issues of banking and lending, practice and procedure. In these difficult times, he is a valuable ally to have on your side."

Richard A. Brownstein

Certified Bankruptcy Specialist
HABERBUSH, LLP
www.lbinsolvency.com
Long Beach, CA

"Richard Hollowell has seen it all throughout his career. Having operated at the highest levels throughout so many real estate cycles make him fully equipped to handle virtually any situation. While there are many that may have similar skill sets, there are few that match his high level of character, integrity, and creativity.

Chris Ganan
MedMen Enterprises
Chief Strategy Officer
www.MedMen.com
Culver City, CA

"I have known Richard for over 30 years. While he was running the Florida office of RER during the S+L debacle of 1989-1993, he and I dealt with multiple assets which we, as the RTC, had assigned to him. In addition to being extremely competent and delivering above average recoveries, Richard was always

honest and forthcoming even during the most difficult situations. He is highly regarded in the industry and I would not hesitate to strongly recommend him."

Henry Lorber
Principal and Founder
Henry Lorber & Associates
www.henrylorberassociates.com
Atlanta, GA

"I have had the pleasure of working closely with Richard Hollowell in a case where our mutual client successfully challenged and defeated an adverse Chapter 11 plan of reorganization and ended up acquiring the real estate assets at issue under favorable terms. Richard is the consummate professional and expert witness. His strategic input, industry expertise, and strongly supported conclusions were integral to the successful outcome."

David Kupetz
Partner
SulmeyerKupetz. P.C.
www.sulmeyerlaw.com
Los Angeles, CA

"Richard Hollowell brought a high level of professionalism, expert advice, and negotiating skills to me in a case with a Special Servicer. I know that with his help I received the best outcome available and that no stone was left unturned by him as he worked through the matter."

Alan Kahn
President
Kahn Development Company
www.kahndevelopment.com
Columbia, SC

"Richard was an expert witness in a real estate matter on behalf of a client involved in a complicated foreclosure, escrow negligence and title insurance battle. The case involved a hurricane, lost documents, a gentleman who went to prison for fraud, and another gentleman who died behind the wheel of his sailboat. A detailed forensic analysis was needed. Richard was extremely helpful and always reliable and available. I recommend that you consider Richard as an expert witness."

Timothy J. Donahue Esq.
Law Offices of Tim Donahue
Orange County, CA

Assignment Highlights

RICHARD K. HOLLOWELL

Real Estate Restructuring/Assignment Highlights

(1971 – 2020)

2019: Engaged by a Los Angeles area municipality and its Community Redevelopment Agency to act as a Settlement Administrator with respect to its obligations to develop certain low-income housing units as a result of a class-action lawsuit brought by members of the local community. Responsibilities included (i) review of building plans and specifications, (ii) oversight of the project planning process, (iii) oversight of the general contractor, (iv) budget preparation, (v) review of project expenditures, (vi) project completion, and (vii) reporting to counsel for the litigants.

2017: Engaged by a major holder of student housing projects to restructure debt associated with a 400-bed project located in Northeast Ohio. Developed alternative restructuring strategies and was responsible for leading all negotiations with a major CMBS Special Servicer.

2015: Engaged by a major holder of student housing projects to restructure the debt associated with a 475-bed project in North Carolina. Developed alternative restructuring strategies and was responsible for leading all negotiations with Freddie Mac, the secured lender.

2014: Participated in raising $25 million from a Florida based family office which contributed to a co-investment joint venture with a highly regarded Southwest Florida land developer. The venture strategy included (i) acquisition and zoning of raw residential land, and (ii) the repositioning of certain stalled residential subdivisions in the Southwest Florida region.

2013: Participated in a raising $50 million which was invested with a major Nevada based developer to facilitate construction and sale of 150 luxury waterfront second homes in Lake Tahoe.

2012: Participated in raising $100 million which was invested with a major real estate opportunity fund with an extensive track record in the acquisition, management, and sale of institutional quality office buildings throughout the U.S. Assigned by the investor to monitor the performance of the acquired properties including financial analysis, budget drift, and strategic decisions made to sell the properties.

2011: Represented a nationally-recognized South Carolina shopping center developer in negotiations with a major Special Servicing entity regarding a large defaulted loan collateralized by a 300,000-power center. Developed alternative restructuring strategies and managed negotiations with the lender to restructure the loan.

2010: Represented a top 20 FDIC-insured bank in evaluating three non-performing AD&C loans in Florida involving (i) 1,800 luxury condominiums, (ii) a downtown land assemblage suited for a 9,000,000 S.F., long-term mixed-use project, and (iii) a mixed-use oceanfront project in the Greater Daytona Beach area. The assignment included the development of alternative exit strategies, financial forecasts, and strategic negotiating recommendations for each property.

2009: Represented a nationally-recognized Kentucky based regional shopping center developer in the out-of-court reorganization of numerous single-purpose real estate entities, and three real estate operating companies. Prepared Chapter 7 liquidation analyses, property valuations, and restructuring proposals; led negotiations with lenders in the interest of avoiding bankruptcy at both the SPE and personal guarantor levels. Properties were located throughout the eastern United States.

2009: Represented an internationally-recognized real estate holding company in the acquisition of Managing Member interests in 12 under-performing multifamily apartment and student housing projects located in nine states. Due diligence and analyses included a review of property level operations, local market conditions, forward-looking projections, capital market considerations and current debt encumbering the properties. Developed strategies to approach seven secured lenders for discounted loan payoffs, and/or modified loan terms and conditions; represented client in lender negotiations, including procurement of replacement financing where necessary.

2008: Represented one of the largest Pension Funds in the world in evaluating the performance and integrity of its major real estate investments on a nationwide basis. Focused on partnership arrangements under which the Pension Fund had committed between $500MM and $2B to the development of urban mixed-use, retail, office and master-planned housing projects.

2008: Represented 10 nationally recognized institutional real estate advisors in performing customized agreed-upon-procedures designed to test the financial and operational performance of various residential real estate projects throughout the western United States.

2007: Acted as a financial intermediary in the arrangement of $35 million of institutional equity to facilitate the acquisition and rehabilitation of a 1.3 million square foot commercial office building in Texas. The mixed-use project included luxury residential condominiums, Class-A office space, upscale spa, retail areas, and related amenities.

2007: Represented a California condominium developer in developing strategies to combat the adverse actions of its construction lender with respect to a residential project plagued by cost overruns, construction delays, out-of-balance conditions as to interest reserves and deteriorating sales conditions. Led negotiations with the bank in the interest of avoiding foreclosure and completing the construction/sellout process.

2007: As a financial intermediary, represented the developer/owner of 3,200 acres of property suited for the development of 6,000 home-sites and 1.5 million square feet of commercial space in raising $30 million of equity to facilitate the property entitlement process and the sale of entitled density to residential homebuilders and commercial developers.

2007: Assisted a bankruptcy trustee in determining the debtors' equity in three land parcels: two located in the Inland Empire and the third, a large planned unit development in suburban Chicago.

2007: Represented a mezzanine lender in developing strategies to maximize recovery of a $12 million loan collateralized by entitled residential land located in California. Development had ceased due to deteriorating market conditions; exit possibilities included (i) sale of the mezzanine lenders position, (ii) foreclosing upon the partnership interests and teaming the lender with a financially capable project developer, (iii) foreclosing upon the partnership interests and placing the entity in a chapter proceeding and/or joint venturing with the adjacent property owner who holds complementary entitlements.

2007: Represented a California residential developer in negotiations with its secured lender with respect to a stalled townhouse project in Orange County.

2007: Solicited potential "vulture buyers" as to the sale and/or recapitalization of a Midwestern luxury homebuilder. Declining residential home sales caused the builder to default on some $100 million of institutional bank debt; such lenders had conceded to accept a payoff at 50% of the principal.

2006: Represented a major property owner responding to a development RFP regarding the development rights to a large riverfront site. The project was to include a festival retail /restaurant component, commercial office buildings and condominium residences. Assisted in determining the appropriate product mix through collaboration with the owner, architectural feasibility analyst; financial modeling; and procurement of debt and equity sufficient to build the project.

2006: Provided advisory services to the owner of strategically located Boca Raton, Florida property suitable for a 1.5 million square foot mixed-use project. Collaborated with architects and feasibility experts on matters including product mix, layout, leasing /sales strategies, and development timelines. Also prepared financial models and joint venture presentations to solicit partners for various project components (condo/hotel; retail/restaurant; office; apartments/condominiums).

2006: Represented the owner of a strategically located riverfront condominium development site in negotiations with a major national condominium developer who sought to purchase the site as part of an assemblage sufficient to support a 2,000-unit project.

2006: Represented a well-known Southeastern-based condominium converter; arranged a $4 million preferred equity loan allowing the developer to effectively finance 97% of costs for a $43 million project in Tampa, Florida.

2005: Participated in a team that served the Southern District Bankruptcy Court as "Plan Administrator," to carry out a Consensual Plan of Reorganization for a bankrupt $125 million high-rise condominium project. As "Plan Administrator," charged with completing construction and sales; dealing with construction defect issues; managing the condominium association; and, reporting to interested parties including the senior lender, mezzanine lender, unsecured creditors and their various counsel.

2005: Acted as a financial intermediary for a major land developer in arranging $25 million of equity financing to facilitate the acquisition, entitlement, and development processes for a 3,000-acre land parcel in northern Florida.

2005: Represented the Official Committee of Unsecured Creditors as a financial advisor while directing forensic investigations with respect to the bankruptcy of a large CLEC telecommunications company. Directed negotiations with secured creditors and made Committee recommendations during the 363-sale process.

2005: Directed the efforts of four forensic accountants in evaluating delay and construction-related damages with respect to a troubled $350MM Performing Arts Center. Evaluation studies assisted counsel in negotiating a master settlement with architects, engineers and general contractors involved in the project.

2005: Provided financial modeling and development underwriting services to the developer of a $300 million mixed-use property in Palm Beach County, Florida. Project components included condominiums, retail, offices, restaurant, condominium offices, and a 1,100-car parking garage. Work product was used to solicit parties interested in joint venturing or purchasing the property assemblage.

2005: Represented the beneficiaries of a Washington D.C. based charitable trust; provided an expert report regarding the likely liquidation value of a major shopping/office complex. The engagement was extended to include "shadow oversight" of the Trustee during his effort to market and sell the property.

2004: Directed a team of real estate, audit, finance, tax, and technology professionals to critically review the operations and financial structure of a major condominium developer. Recommendations resulted in the developer streamlining its accounting procedures, upgrading information systems, improving investor communications and establishing human resource and loan compliance departments.

2004: Consulted for the developer of a $400 million luxury mixed-use hotel, condominium, and condominium hotel oceanfront project. Advice extended to issues including unit mix, unit size, pricing, and project amenities while assisting the developer in selecting other professionals including, lawyers, feasibility analysts, engineers, general contractors and luxury hotel management companies.

2004: Engaged by a group of limited partners to investigate the actions of a general partner responsible for acquiring, managing, and leasing ten commercial properties. Identified certain aggressive actions of the general partner and quantified potential damages. Work product led to "wind-up" negotiations between the parties.

2004: Originated and negotiated acquisition financing on behalf of a developer actively involved in the development of a mixed-use project in Key West, Florida. The presentation included loan underwriting criteria, financial model, development timetable, and market analysis, all used by the bank as the core document leading to loan approval.

2004: Assisted a development company in determining the fair market ground rent applicable to a development site suited for the expansion of a major hospital. Work was instrumental in heading-off potential litigation with governing municipal agencies and led to a tax-free trade of the property.

2004: Assisted a municipality in determining the prospective internal rate of return attendant to a proposed long-term ground lease of commercial oceanfront property. The report was featured at public hearings where proposed vertical development was debated.

2003: Directed the out of court reorganization of a major aviation training company. Negotiated a $12 million reduction in the secured lenders $19 million loans. Assisted in identifying and negotiating with a merger partner, as well as in procuring new debt. Directed the successful reorganization of a related aviation parts company through the settlement of adverse litigation which had led to its bankruptcy filing.

2003: Provided financial modeling services to the developer of a $100 million mixed-use project abutting a major sports complex. The financial model was used by the developer to negotiate a complex loan facility involving both construction and permanent commitments.

2003: Assisted a School Board in evaluating potential claims against architects and project managers involved in a $40 million school project. Counsel for the School Board used our expert report as a core document when bringing negligence actions against the professionals.

2003: Established a relationship with a $5 billion Japanese company to conduct acquisition due diligence with respect to their U.S. based acquisition program. Directed acquisition due diligence team in evaluating nine targeted companies with aggregate sales exceeding $1.1 billion.

2002: Directed the merger of a major seafood distribution company operating in Chapter 11 bankruptcy, with a complimentary competitor from New York. Identified over 350 possible merger candidates; developed and circulated a Request for Proposal; actively negotiated with 15 qualified parties; negotiated contract terms and employment agreements; participated in creditor negotiations; and, assisted in the preparation of a Chapter 11 Plan of Reorganization.

2002: Evaluated the real estate portfolio of a private individual who owns and/or controls 20 major commercial properties in Florida; developed a plan and recommendation for an interrupted condominium development providing alternative strategies under which the development could be completed or liquidated at maximum value.

2001: Expert testimony provided in a developer vs. developer lawsuit. Reviewed and evaluated a projection of lost profits prepared by the plaintiff's expert. The projection was prepared to support the claim of a local homebuilder whose earnings on the development of 300 homes were far below his expectations. The scope also considered analyzing all aspects of the homebuilder's product offerings, marketing methods, and financing arrangements, as well as the due diligence performed by the homebuilder prior to his purchase of lots.

2000: Conducted property search, analysis, and evaluation of over 50 properties leading to a purchase contract involving an anchored retail center, in connection with a 1031 exchange as an advisor to a major law firm.

1999: Negotiated leverage buyout and secured financing for a $20 million aviation landing gear business.

1999: Negotiated the acquisition of non-performing institutional debt encumbering the assets of a Florida based aeronautical repair station on behalf of a South Florida business entrepreneur.

1992-1998: As Managing Director of a nationally recognized real estate asset management firm and President of its five operating subsidiaries, directed 175 full-time employees and 200 subcontractors in five offices (Washington, D.C., New York City, Dallas, Boca Raton, Newport Beach, CA) in (i) the evaluation, management and disposition of more than 1,000 non-performing real estate-related assets with an aggregate balance of $1.6 billion, (ii) pre-securitization mortgage loan due diligence on hundreds of commercial real estate properties, (iii) a multi-million joint venture with the FDIC regarding the collection of judgment deficiency and charge-off accounts, (iv) management of numerous receiverships involving commercial real estate foreclosures totaling $500 million, and (v) underwriting of real estate acquisitions and conduit loans on behalf of Salomon Brothers, TransAtlantic Capital, Citicorp Securities, Chase Securities, Goldman Sachs and Credit Suisse First Boston and (vi) directed so-called special servicing assignments for third parties.

1992: Testified on behalf of the RTC/FDIC in Federal Court in an action brought by a Limited Partnership. The partnership claimed significant damages caused by the RTC who repudiated seven master leases of a large savings institution, on office buildings sold to the partnerships. In addition to damages alleged due to lease repudiation, the partnership claimed additional damages due to the RTC's alleged failure to maintain the properties during their tenancy.

1992: Assisted in forming the first Community Development Tax District in Osceola County, Florida (prior to Disney's City of Celebration) to facilitate the acquisition and development of a troubled 1,000-acre golf course community. The project had been the subject of a seven-year contested foreclosure and related bankruptcy.

1991: Appointed by the Circuit Court as receiver of a 350,000 Sq. Ft. oceanfront festival retail project. Negotiated a master settlement agreement between the syndicated partnership, lender, and interested tenants, thereafter selling the project on behalf of the lender.

1990: Represented a major insurance company in directing the orderly redevelopment and sale of Palm Court Plaza, a 130,000-square foot, mixed-use project located in Palm Beach County, Florida.

1989: Conceived and directed the formation of Florida's first Commercial Community Development District; the District was used as a financing vehicle to effect a $70 million loan workout with a major New York bank on a 628-acre commercial/industrial park.

1988: Directed the analysis, underwriting, and orderly disposition of the $100 million Broadway Plaza, mixed-use project in downtown Denver, Colorado.

1988: Led a team of 19 professionals in the analysis of Broadview Savings and Loan, a $2 billion savings association located in Cleveland, Ohio. Engaged by a Chicago based conglomerate who sought to acquire the institution. Developed "going concern" and "liquidation" valuation models, recommended bid price and overall negotiation strategy to be used in negotiations with the FSLIC.

1984-1986: Negotiated over $100 million of whole loan swaps relating to 12 real estate loans made by two saving associations involved in financing properties on Hilton Head Island. Provided testimony over a period of seven years on behalf of the FSLIC in its pursuit of recovery from bank officers, appraisers, and law firms involved in financing properties. Negotiated the sale of various non-performing loans, residential development properties and golf courses to third parties, liquidating certain interests of the failed institutions. Directed the orderly workout and disposition of four historic adaptive-reuse projects on behalf of an insured savings institution. The aggregate value of the properties approximated $75 million and included projects located in Chattanooga, Tennessee, Macon, Georgia, Atlanta, Georgia, and Raleigh, North Carolina.

1983: Directed the workout and sale of six residential development projects located throughout Florida on behalf of an insured savings institution.

1982: Participated in the successful syndication and rehabilitation of Old Knoxville City Hall, a 65,000-square-foot public building built-in 1845. Master leased the building to the Tennessee Valley Authority. Managed the project refinancing process in 1990 and 1997.

1980-1981: Participated in the development of several commercial real estate projects on behalf of one of the largest regional shopping mall developers in the world, including (i) United Artist Cinema, Charleston, South Carolina, (ii) Shopko anchored strip-center, Madison, Wisconsin, (iii) 240 room Holiday Inn Hotel, Cincinnati, Ohio, and (iv) various restaurant, bank and freestanding retail buildings throughout the eastern United States.

1979: Foreclosed, redesigned, built and sold, a 176-unit townhome project in Sunrise, Florida on behalf of a major credit company.

1978: Developed through a joint venture, an 800 lot second home community located in Vero Beach, Florida on behalf of a major credit company. As part of the project, developed a private water and sewer utility that was ultimately sold to a public entity.

1977: Foreclosed, redesigned, built, and sold a 320-unit condominium project located in Coral Springs, Florida on behalf of a major credit company.

1976: Foreclosed, rehabilitated, and sold a 100-unit waterfront condominium project located on the Intracoastal Waterway in Palm Beach County, Florida, on behalf of a major credit company.

1975: Foreclosed and completed the development of a 300-pad mobile home project in Marion, Illinois for one of America's top-10 banks.

1974: Foreclosed, completed construction stabilized cash flow, and sold a 400-unit multifamily project in Dallas, Texas for one of America's top-10 banks.

1973: Foreclosed, completed construction, installed hotel management, stabilized cash flow, and sold two budget motels in Orlando, Florida (256 rooms) and Newport Richey, Florida (128 rooms) for one of America's top-10 banks.

1973: Foreclosed, completed construction stabilized cash flow, and sold a 320-unit multifamily project in Wichita, Kansas for one of America's top-10 banks.

Made in United States
Cleveland, OH
05 November 2026

47665210R00050